MASTER WITHIN

Passion for Life

MASTER CHEN
YUN XIANG TSENG

Dear Brian & Ashely

Return to Simplicity

Live your true nature

May the Tao bless

Yuxiang Tseng

4/9/13

in the garden Publishing

a media company of
WHAT WOULD LOVE DO INT'L LTD

ISBN: 978-0-9855314-5-4
Library of Congress data available upon request.

Cover and Interior Design by Christine Horner

Published by:
IN THE GARDEN PUBLISHING
P.O. Box 752252
Dayton, OH 45475

www.inthegardenpublishing.com
www.whatwouldlovedointl.com

TABLE OF CONTENTS

Editor's Note

Master Within may be a book that brings Eastern philosophy into focus for a wider audience, but it is also a book that adheres to a long authorial and literary tradition. Before there was what we now call literary fiction, before novels and other recreational writing proliferated, there were books written as journals and travelogues, histories and biographies, precautionary tales and stories of exemplary lives. Even the earliest novels in the English language pretended to be true stories so that those reading them would not be accused of wasting their time on imaginary writing.

Although the idea of creating fictitious characters created purely for recreational reading grew, the tradition of creating a "public persona" as part of a non-fiction work remained a popular motif. Hence, no less than Benjamin Franklin, in his own "true" autobiography, embellished his life to help set a better example for his readers. George Washington benefited greatly in reputation from the stories invented by Mason Locke Weems, who essentially just attached George Washington's name to fictional tales of "virtue" which would provide good examples for citizens young and old.

Master Chen is no less desirous of creating a clear, readable and enjoyable narrative. To carry forward the lessons he has devoted a life to learning and to assist his readers in attaining their own mastery, he has combined events from his own life, his childhood, family, education and the tests that he faced, together with a tale of a young man called to higher purpose and power. By creating a character whose adventures help teach us all, Master Chen becomes the young boy who is called to greatness, overcomes all obstacles, and rises to a state of high mastery.

Allow yourself to become that young boy, to become the novitiate, the initiate, the student and ultimately your own master. Find, focus, channel and champion your chi. You have a master within.

Preface

Immortal Grand Master, *Cheng Yu Li* (r),
lovingly known as Master *Li* (circa 1930)

    I was born into a very poor family in the humble village of
Chang Le City in Fujian Province located in the southeast corner
of China. Chang Le means, "The longest happiness." Though

we were a modest family we enjoyed life, we enjoyed the way that we lived.

From the age of six, I was chosen to live and cultivate in the *Taoist* Temples of *Wu Dang* Mountain, China. It is there that I learned and lived the ancient, five-thousand-year-old secrets of a happy, long and fulfilling life. *Wu Dang* Mountain is one of China's most sacred mountains. It is one of the birthplaces of *Taoism.* Everything is mystical about Wu Dang, where the sky opens to fields of immortality. A magical mist nourishes treasures of herbal pharmacology. Fifty thousand years of human civilization trace to the area. Seventy-two mountain peaks bow like flames inward toward the main peak. Looking from above, the main peak resembles a turtle sitting in balance on top of the fire. Little wonder that, in *Taoist* philosophy, only the turtle, representative of the water element, can sit on top to balance the extreme fire of the universe.

Recently, I journeyed back to a remote cave in the *Wu Dang* Mountains of China to once again rediscover the purpose of living, going back to the root of life there and reconnecting with the spirit of the people and the mountain. For thirty days, I retreated to a cave, with no baggage. Everything was simple for me. This retreat pulled me back to my origins in order to rediscover the true spirit, to find stillness. We all have to find our own cave daily, devoting our self completely to turning inward to discover our true heart. God, or *Tao*, is always delivering gold and joy, always delivering selflessly. If your heart is not open, then God is not able to deliver. Just as a gardener must find suitable soil in which to grow seeds, so too must *Tao* find suitable mud to grow the golden lotus.

Life is a journey. We come to this existence to enjoy life as opposed to being entertained by life. We come into life and we will go from life with nothing in the material. All we have is the glory and joy of living in this short journey. Being human is a gift of *Tao*. As humans, we all have emotions and desires. We are the combination of our material and spiritual life. We must each entertain and enjoy life in our own unique ways. On our journey, we must find a way to balance both our material and the spiritual being to make the best of life. In this book, you the reader can learn the method to enjoy, understand and respect your emotions and desires. This book guides you toward learning a way to live passionately with yourself and others.

Tao follows what is nature and then unites with heaven as one. This is the core philosophy of Taoism. Through my own personal experience as a *Taoist* priest, I explain the Taoist philosophy of life in a very practical way. By looking at life from another way, I hope to provide you an understanding that life is a joyful journey. We are each the creator and entertainer of our own personal, joyful lives.

Taoism spans over five thousand years of history but still, Western society has received few clear explanations and has only a limited understanding of practical *Taoist* philosophy. Very few people in Western culture know about and truly understand Taoism. For many reasons, not the least of which are philosophical and language barriers, Taoism has remained shrouded in mystery for Westerners.

I began my training as a Taoist priest at the age of six. I was honorably chosen to be part of a five-thousand-year-old Taoist lineage by my immortal Grand Master, *Cheng Yu Li*, lovingly known as Master *Li*. I was chosen to carry on this sacred tradition and to bring this wisdom to the West. I have lived in the United States for over twenty years now, learning the culture and making friends with thousands of people. I have gained some access to the way to communicate these Taoist concepts to people from the West. I was designated, by my master, as liaison between East and West to explain the mystical secrets of life. I am here to share with you and entertain you with this ancient knowledge.

I don't expect people to believe everything that I say. I merely present this knowledge of Tao from my own understanding of nearly forty years of practicing Taoism, so that people in the West can, perhaps use this philosophy in their own personal and intellectual discussions. I am the ambassador and messenger of the ancient *Tao* to the modern world of the West and I offer you this book to introduce a way to understand the mystical meaning of life and to answer some of the basic questions of mankind; the basic questions that all religions try to answer.

Happiness is the only purpose of life. Taoism introduces to humans a very practical way to live a happy life. I introduce to you this way of understanding and cultivating life, to transcend ordinary life, thereby becoming an extraordinary human. We all continue to grow into heaven. We live our heaven every day. There is no physical heaven or hell; it is in living that we create these concepts. We are not here to suffer from past karma or to redeem our "sins." We are only here to find the true value, dignity and respect of life. We are here to rebuild the connection between our personal "heaven and earth."

We are here to balance and harmonize everyday life. Everyone has free access to the gateway to return home. The access to this gateway begins with learning to enjoy life—today and at this very moment.

Acknowledgement

My Heartfelt Thanks

I extend my most profound thanks to my master Li, Cheng Yu who chose me to be her student and patiently taught me the traditions and wisdom of the Tao. Through master Li, I learned the unique healing arts of the Long Men sect. Master Li's vision of the world was one of harmony and unity. To help realize this vision, she sent me to the Western world with the mission to share the Taoist teachings of virtue, health, and harmony.

In this regard, I am a messenger for thousands of years of Taoism wisdom. I did not create this wisdom or the healing methods I teach. I am simply a conduit of them.

To my family in China who support me and trust in me, especially my parents who gave their blessing for me to follow the Taoist path, I give my deepest thanks.

My wife, Tiffany Phillips, is not only a life companion but also one of the wisest persons I have met. Tiffany's wholehearted support and unshakable trust strengthens and inspires me as a teacher and a human being. My beautiful children Lillian, Hsing, and Kai selflessly give me to the world; they never complain about how little time I have for them. I am a lucky daddy.

I have an abiding appreciation for the people of Long Island, New York. When I first arrived in the United States, they provided the support that helped me start teaching and learn about American life. Among these special people are David B. Axelrod, Gerald Luglio, Roland Kaupp and his lovely wife Gesena, Reuben Starishevsky, Richard Hirsch, Helen Miller and Marie Korn.

For the past 20 years, many sincere and dedicated people have been instrumental in helping to organize my seminars and classes. For their invaluable support and hard work my heartfelt thanks go to Kristina Naldjian, Corinne Chaves, Susan Ross, Cynthia O'Donnell, Tim Breuwer, Nicholas Schnell, Ken Baker, Raymond Solis, Colleen Herman, Rosie Coelho, Rhonda Louie, Karen Atkin, and Alan Holt. The earnest efforts of these people have ensured that I have had the platforms from which I could teach Taoist healing arts and philosophy. They continue to enable me to bring Taoist teachings to your door step.

How can I ever adequately thank my dear friend Robert Olsen. It was Robert who literally helped bring this book to life. Robert spent countless hours assembling and editing mountains of notes and records from my many lectures. To help me on my mission to share Taoism with the West, Robert spent five years living in my house to help take care of my family. I am deeply indebted to Robert for his kindness.

I am very grateful to my loyal assistant Kristina Naldjian, who has been with me since 2003. She has helped me organize my seminars, business, and personal matters. Kristina is one of those close to me who is a true practitioner of Taoism.

A wonderful friend, disciple, and wise man is Reuben Starishevsky from Huntington, New York. Reuben is a trusted counselor who has guided me like both a father and a friend.

After I first arrived in the United States, Reuben made a special effort to help me learn about American life and customs. His assistance also was vitally important in editing and publishing this book. Reuben supports my mission with unflagging enthusiasm and has traveled with me back to Wu Dang Mountain ten times. He makes my teaching in the United States a joy and infuses me with passion.

I am uniquely fortunate to have found a special brother in Jimmy Salvagio, who has given me so much support and encouragement to share Taoist philosophy and health practices.

Finally, I want to express my deepest appreciation to the many hundreds of other students and friends in America who have loyally supported me. It is because of them that I can be a teacher and share the precious Way of the Tao.

Introduction

People can become their own personal spiritual sage and discover their "Master Within." It depends on your determination, discipline and dedication. If you possess this motivation, then you can cultivate spiritual enlightenment just as easily in your home as you can in a remote temple. Though your human existence is in the earthly, mortal world, your heart transcends beyond the mortal and into the heavenly, spiritual realm.

From the mud grows the golden lotus. This book is a facilitating procedure for moving from an old unhappy self to your new inspired passionate self. It provides a method for getting out of the mud you and others have created for yourself, a method for re-creating yourself. In a very real and tangible sense, this procedure will help you to reincarnate yourself. By recognizing and changing self-defeating life patterns you can develop a new model of nurturing, healing and spiritual growth.

This book teaches procedures for how to process. Process life and be the master of your life rather than a victim of life. Make conscious choices in life rather than have those choices dictated for you. Learn to look at life as challenging and entertaining rather than being entertained or frightened by life. You can sit around lamenting how life is not fair to you, or you can engage and be a full partner in life. The choice is yours!

Engage in life rather than be engaged by life. That is to say, make conscious choices in your life rather than have choices unconsciously made for you. Create a sacred space for yourself and let go of the external and internal guards and masks that may have been put upon you as a child, but now continue to be unconsciously worn by you as an adult. Help others, as they will help you, to process through the guard and mask. Carry no discrimination towards others and do not judge others. Instead, learn from them and help them along. Learn the skills of self-mastery so that, when you live your everyday life, you will not be dirtied or polluted by the mud that surrounds you.

Stillness is a companion of emotion. You need, merely, to pause in your life, pause your worried thoughts, to recognize how stillness helps to process emotions and thereby, let them go. Unfortunately, people often times act to the contrary. They hold on tightly to their thoughts, cementing their emotions into hardened bodies. This book provides an opportunity to pause your life and to lick the wounds so that you can move on to the comforting and healing energy that stillness offers. "Master Within" provides a process where you can break out of your existing mold, out of your comfort zone, and in so doing, do something extraordinary. Become an extraordinary human. Everyday life is a major obstacle to breaking through the alchemy of our existence. Yet, everyday life allows great opportunities to break through to cultivate human and spiritual energy. Be willing to see two sides of the coin and then, perhaps, you will see three, four and five sides of the coin!

In order to properly and fully attach, one must first learn how to detach. The object is to do nothing, so to speak, but leave nothing undone. Taoism is a way of living to do just that. Do nothing, but leave nothing undone. Taoism is a philosophy foremost, a way of life not a religion. People of all religious beliefs can benefit from a Taoist way of life. Taoism maintains that a true teacher is also always a student. To be a good teacher, one must be an extraordinary student.

I am asking you to ride a dragon. You must first have the guts, resources and fortitude to ride this dragon. Next, you must take care to make sure that your butt sticks to the dragon. It will be a rough ride, and the dragon will try to throw you for a loop at every chance, so make sure that your butt is stuck to the dragon. Once you are stuck to the dragon, make the effort to feel the flow of the ride. You won't, at first, know how to drive the dragon, so feel the flow of the ride. Finally, enjoy your ride; go with the ride. Don't try to fight the ride. Be one with the dragon and enjoy it. The dragon is representative of spirit, so if you want to ride the dragon, you must become spirit. To do this you must have pure heavenly spirit—*Yuan Shen*. You must purify the mind; work with the mind to quiet it. Form the golden elixir of eternal life by transmuting the bodily essence or seed of life (*Jing*) to vapor energy (*Qi*), transmuting *Qi* to spirit (*Shen*), cultivating *Shen* to the void and returning the void to *Tao* or God.

This book is designed to train you to become a wise driver. The question posed to you is, "Are you qualified to ride the dragon?" Learn to enjoy emotions and not suffer from them. Learn to find unity from contradictions. Learning to find unity from contradictions is *Tao*. Learn to see what you don't immediately see, in addition to what you do see. Taoist philosophy is about teaching a totally practical way of living. It's school smart and street smart.

PART I

Who Am I?

Chapter 1

Do You Know Who You Are?

My ma tells me that in my early years, until I was the age of three, I didn't speak a single word. Because of this, my parents worried that I was deaf, and so they took me to countryside doctors to have me checked. In the end, there was nothing wrong with me. I can only guess that I just did not want to speak for my first three years. Although I didn't talk, I was always observing, learning to know myself, to know my world and to know my place in my world. After my first three years, once I started to talk, my ma says that I couldn't stop. As soon as I started to talk, I became known throughout the countryside as a medium, able to speak for the spirit world. People from all over the village and city, perhaps thousands of people came to me to ask questions. I became somewhat famous. Being a medium caused some health concerns for me. To speak those languages, to act as a medium requires your pre-heaven energy and that can deteriorate your post-heaven physical health.

I ask, "Do you really know and understand who you are?" Ask yourself, "Does a transient guest in a hotel carry any loyalty towards that hotel? Do you not want to enjoy the quality of the hotel as though it were your own home?" When you find the true sacred connection to the "hotel" of your body you will then find the true meaning of "Who Am I?" A guest at a hotel merely checks in for the material comfort, but someone who is truly connected, or has ownership in the hotel, takes the time necessary to appreciate and know that hotel. Guests just check in and out, but when you find that loyal connection, you will check in with fondness and nurturing toward the hotel, and find the true meaning of "Who am I."

When I was between three and six years of age, our community had a small Taoist temple located deep inside our village, down by the brook. The temple had a few female priests and three to five male priests. The village people would all go there to ask for wisdom. The priests also carried out Taoist services. The three main priests at the temple all liked me very much, so I went there often to spend time, to pray, light incense and watch the spirits. I talked to the priests about metaphysical arts, metaphysical theory and other mystical things like that. One of the masters in the temple—she didn't have a name so she called herself "Nameless"—always taught me that I had a special destiny and that I would be chosen to go to Wu Dang Mountain. I had heard of the Wu Dang name but did not know what it was about at the time. So it was that, almost from birth, my true heavenly spirit, the *Yuan Shen*, was allowed to follow its essential nature.

We must all be truthful to find our essential nature. It's necessary to be honest about one's self to allow the true spirit a chance to reassert itself. Dishonesty creates attachments to post-heaven judgments and ego, empowering the human intelligent spirit while driving the true spirit away. The true spirit must care about this body, care about this hotel and this life in order to have loyalty to its existence.

Pretend, at least for now, that everyone knows your thoughts. Everyone knows what you think, how you think and that perhaps they are judged by you. Practice this, because even though your conscious mind and their conscious mind may not be aware of the thoughts and judgments, your and their true spirit is indeed aware and affected. This practice is the first step leading you to become true to your spirit or essential nature. This technique is the first step in leading you to the three treasures of Tao—conscience, mercy and forgiveness. As with any process of changing old thoughts and behaviors, this practice will be challenging, so make it a fun learning experience and know that we all will occasionally fall on our butt while testing our new training wheels. When you do fall, remember to gracefully apply the third treasure of Tao by practicing forgiveness towards yourself. Lick the wounds, forgive yourself and move on while saying, "I can do it." Knowing all along that "enough is enough" brings the greatest happiness.

The question "Who am I?" historically has been a mystery. Humans of every religion and of every culture look for this answer. Humans have written the Bible, the Taoist canon and the Koran. All of these and more were written and translated by humans, interpreted by humans. Mankind never stops using its own intelligence to research this mystery, to solve this mystery. The more we research, the more we try to solve the mystery, the bigger the mystery becomes. As a result, mankind becomes more confused. Some maniacal people take advantage of this confusion by using their extreme thinking and using their extreme preference to impose their own will on all of mankind. For this reason, the world is always waging wars in the name of the God, from ancient times to present times. People use arms and power to dominate the world in order to lend power to their own belief, no matter of how twisted that belief may be.

This type of mentality has confused and mistranslated the world of God for thousands of years. Politics and religion have always combined and with that people always try to dominate each other, control each other, murder each other and destroy the lives of each other. At birth, humans have a primordial mind and a pure soul that becomes polluted by this train of thought. The sacred connection between man and God, between man and immortals, is damaged.

The *Tao* that can be taught is not eternal. The name that can be named is not eternal. The greatest wisdom, the man who shows the greatest wisdom, is the one who doesn't talk. Those who know don't talk; those who talk the most, don't know. Taoism is one of the oldest philosophical practices of the human mind. Taoism is the concentrated record of ancient people. It records our ancient people's thinking. It is the unity of all religions in the world. The book, *Tao Te Ching*, is a record of all the answers for the human world. It is a very simple book; yet, it describes the path of humans including their origin, the growing, the aging, dying and on to the rebirth. All the theory, technique and explanation has been encompassed within this book. So in our book, *Master Within*, we try, from a Taoist point of view, to translate the concept of "Who Am I?" Rather than continue to confuse people with thoughtful, modern explanations, modern scientific explanations of "Who am I?" we try to make it very simple to get back to the origin of the question. We go back to the original concept of our ancestors to reunite man and God. To answer the question "Who am I?" we explain the concepts of *Jing*, *Qi* and *Shen*, an energetic way of understanding the human body. We explain the content of the human body, every part of the *Jing*, *Qi*, and *Shen* in the human body, with focus then placed on *Shen* or spirit. We do this so as to give you recognition that God is within man. This is the relationship between *Yuan Shen* the original God spirit and *Shi Shen* the human intelligent spirit. Very simply put, you follow nature to death and you reverse nature to immortality or God. Tell people "I am who I am." I am human; yet, I am God at the same time.

Chapter 2

Concepts of Jing, Qi and Shen

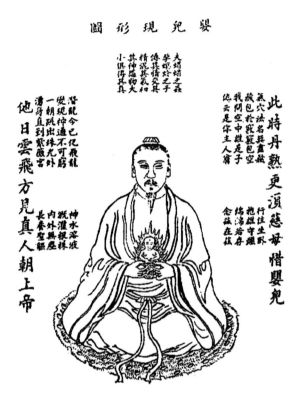

Because I was a medium, a conduit between the post-heaven, physical world and the pre-heaven, spiritual world, from a very early age, this practice caused me some serious health concerns. In order to speak those languages between the two realms, to act as a medium requires the use of pre-heaven energy. As a result, the practice can deteriorate your post-heaven, physical health. So it was, between the ages of three and six years old, that I had a weak body and was very sick. Poor nutrition may have also contributed to the poor health. Regardless of my physical health, I was always happy. I always continued to serve with my gifts and I never complained. People came and I always spoke. I was called a "spooky" child.

Jing, *Qi*, and *Shen* are the human energetic structure, the basic materials of the human body. *Jing*, *Qi*, and *Shen* are the three treasures or jewels of our human bodies. In *Taoism*, good health and longevity in age are attained through cultivation and refinement of these three treasures of our body. When we are in our mother's womb, these three energies are uncontaminated by earthly attachments and expectations. In this pure or pre-heaven form the three treasures are known as original generative essence, original vapor-energy and original spiritual-energy.

Jing is the essence of our life, the generative energy, the seed of life. It is the bodily fluid, the treasure of eternal life, hard to produce, yet easy to waste. Every organ has its own *Jing*, and this *Jing* from every organ, gathers at the eyes. *Jing* has two expressions in our human body. *Yin Jing* comes from the food and water we consume and has its origin in the heart and includes the blood of the body. *Yang Jing* is the first brick in the house of our creation. It comes to each of us through a transmutation process from the spleen, on to the *Ren* channel and then into the ovaries and testicles; which are its origin. *Yang Jing* consists of the reproductive fluids or the seed of life. Pure *Yang Jing* is the source for creating new life. Recent scientific research substantiates this claim in an entirely new way, showing that human sperm can be used to create new generative growth of all organs, much like the human stem cell, but perhaps even better.

By reversing what is human nature, unfettered sex and emotion; and through cultivating stillness in the human body by losing expectations and attachments, *Yang Jing* or pre-heaven *Jing*, is transmuted to pre-heaven or spiritual *Qi*, and *Yin Jing* is transmuted to post-heaven or bodily *Qi*.

Qi is the vital life force or vapor-energy of our human body. It can be likened to the gasoline that fuels all our action and expression. As with *Jing*, *Qi* has two forms. *Yuan Qi* or pre heaven *Qi* resides in the kidneys and originally comes to you from your parents, but it can also be transmuted from *Yang Jing*. The second form of *Qi* is Zhen *Qi* or post-heaven *Qi*. Zhen *Qi* is both *Yin* and *Yang* at birth and is derived from the air you breathe, the food you eat and the water that you consume. As we age, *Yin* and *Yang Qi* generally move out of balance. One must rebalance the Zhen *Qi* to gain immortality, and a healthy and long-lived life. If you follow human nature though, and you continue to let *Yuan Qi* in the kidneys dissipate, you will die. That is one reason why all major religions tell you to be as a child. It means to reverse what is nature, cultivate your energies to their pre-heaven form, end the cycle of reincarnation and become the immortal master within.

The third treasure, *Shen*, is spiritual energy and it is in charge of human wisdom and intelligence. The *Shen* is original spirit and intelligent spirit combined. We come to this world with original spirit but then as we age we gain intelligent spirit to maintain every day activity. *Shen* determines the quality of life regarding whether to live or to die, whereas; *Qi* decides the quality of everyday life. *Shen* decides the absolute destination of human life. If *Shen,* or original spirit, stays in the body you live, if it leaves you die. We are the spirit. *Shen,* or spiritual energy, is formless and can be channeled to the internal organs for healing purposes. As with *Jing* and *Qi,* *Shen* also has two forms. *Yuan Shen* is the original spiritual energy of *Tao* or God, and *Shi Shen* is the spirit of intelligence. When we are first born the original spirit, *Yuan Shen,* is in charge but as we age, spirit of intelligence, *Shi Shen,* tries to dominate the human body, causing many of the physical, psychological and spiritual problems that we experience as adults.

Together, *Jing, Qi,* and *Shen* form the three treasures of the human body. Just as a hotel is not a hotel until you have a guest, *Jing, Qi,* and *Shen* make the hotel of the human body. *Jing, Qi,* and *Shen* explain the hotel and guest structure. Through these three treasures, the mundane breath is transformed into spiritual energy. *Jing* and *Qi* are comparable to the hotel, or the water that grows a fish, and *Shen* is can be likened to the guest, or the fish. Each human has a certain quality and quantity of pre-heaven *Qi.* If you collect, nurture and cultivate a great quality of water, that is, a great quality of *Jing* and *Qi,* then this will make for a happy fish, or spiritual energy that is long-lived. Through life's journey humans can either increase or decrease the quantity and quality of *Jing* and *Qi.* Lust for material things decreases the quality and longevity of life, along with the sacred power of the *Shen,* whereas becoming a "Master Within" increases the quality and quantity of *Jing* and *Qi* and the sacred power of the *Shen.*

Being spooky and my ability to communicate between two worlds may be the reason that my Master *Li* was able to tap into the secret communication channel that led her to ask my future Kung Fu Master, *Guo Gao Yi,* the Kung Fu abbot from Wu Dang

Mountain, to travel thousands of miles to come get me. On July 12, my birthday, Master *Li* gave *Guo Gao Yi* exact instructions on where to find me, how I would be dressed, what I would look like, and where to look for me. At the time, I was a little "cowboy," tending and taking my cow to the mountain during the day. One day, I had my lone cow by the brook when, all of a sudden, I raised my head to see a very mystical man with a long beard, wearing a funny hat, making strange, flowing movements in slow motion—what I now know as *Tai Chi*. Master *Guo* held both palms facing each other, moving his hands as if he were playing with a ball. When he abruptly flicked this imaginary ball into a tree branch the whole branch shook, along with the leaves that fell to the ground. I was startled, but I was also a curious young boy, so I came forward to ask the old man, "*Tao Zhang*," (respected Taoist priest) I said, "Could you please tell me what kind of magic you do? What special power makes the tree shake?" The Taoist priest patted me on the head, looked into my eyes and said, "I have been looking for you. There is someone who sent me to look for you. I will teach you and show you the magic power of what I am doing." I was totally enraptured, so I replied, "Yes, of course I want to see it, I want to learn!" The master said, "It is very far away. Do you think that you will be able to do it? Are you sure you want to go?" I answered, "Of course I want to go." I wanted to learn the secrets to reversing the energy of nature, to cultivate the *Jing* and the *Qi*, to transmute them to *Shen*, the spiritual special energy. Soon, I will tell you how I was allowed to go.

When *Yang Jing* or sexual energy pumps at the gate of *Yang* and it breaks the gate of Tao then there is the creation of a human being, but if the *Yang Jing* is reversed through cultivation of stillness, *Jing* is then transmuted to *Qi*. This method of reversing *Yang Jing* from breaking the gate has to be taught by a master.

Cultivation and refinement of *Jing*, *Qi*, and *Shen* are an essential link in finding and becoming the master of your own. Through cultivating stillness in the human body and mind; letting go of attachments, desires and emotions, and through living a virtuous life, we are able to open our hearts to the gifts that *Tao* or God showers upon us. Through cultivating stillness, we are able to know and appreciate who we are. It is very important to know that the human body is an absolutely necessary component in cultivating stillness and living virtuously, so be accepting of who and where you are in your life. Be accepting of the fact that you are a human with a human body.

Chapter 3

The Material Self

My father was an uneducated farmer who was not so wise.
He was just an average farmer who had always been called foolish
by the whole village. We were the weakest family in the village.
As a result, my family was often times physically abused by other
families. People hit my parents and many times, my father was

injured. At the time, somewhere in my small-child heart, I thought to myself, "I will go away and learn all the Kung Fu skills and one day come back to my village and knock everybody out. Then they won't dare to look down at my family any longer."

Parallel to this, my ma was looked upon by many other families as one of the best women in the village, always giving advice, always giving help, never branding anyone, never hating anyone. Some people looked at her as a role model for women. She was a wise, loving person who balanced my family. My mother gave to me my first lessons of humanity: forgive, love, have compassion and live with joy at being poor and weak. She told me that being weak was the best protection for our family. We were so weak that we posed no threat to other families, enabling us to always survive. She taught me to give what we could give; use only what we needed and give the rest away.

Shi Shen, the spirit of intelligence and master of the material self, is also the administrator of all the organs. It relates to all the emotions and physical desires. The Shi Shen is supported by Yin Jing and post-heaven Qi. Shi Shen collects, processes and creates information about the world, both inside and outside of you. How truthful that information is depends on how truthful you are to your original, heavenly spirit or Yuan Shen. Shi Shen starts from complete innocence at birth and evolves until it gains extreme intelligence through the journey of life. Most humans, perhaps ninety-eight percent, base living entirely upon their Shi Shen or intelligent spirit; depending entirely on physical and emotional desires to dictate their lives. This dependence upon physical and emotional desires leads to suffering of stress and disease, producing a low quality of life and early death. Material intelligence, as you might imagine, is often jaded by our very limited perceptions of the world around us.

As an illustration, in ancient times there were six blind men. Each was asked to describe an elephant. The first blind man was in front of the elephant. He stood to feel the trunk of the elephant and in so doing he declared, "An elephant is long and flowing like a snake." The second man touched his palm to the ear of the elephant and exclaimed, "An elephant is flat and broad like a giant leaf." A third blind man stroked one of the elephant's rough legs and determined, "It is tall and straight like a tree covered in bark." The fourth man wisped his hand over the eyelashes of the elephant and assured everyone that, "An elephant is like a wispy broom." A fifth blind man felt the tail and decided that, "An elephant is very much like a whip." And finally, the sixth blind man felt the belly of the elephant and announced, "An elephant is broad and round like the earth." Each man was limited by his narrow exposure to the elephant and was only able to describe what he had understood. Each description was limited by each man's restricted perceptions. Don't let your own blindfold keep you from knowing the world. Be open to knowing the world in many different ways.

Similarly, a frog that sat at the bottom of a deep well, spoke with a bird that had flown in to sit on the edge of the well. In their conversation, the frog described the sky to be as wide across as the well. The bird retorted, "In no way are you right. The sky is much wider." The frog said knowingly, "I have lived here, in this well, all of my life and never has the sky been broader than the width of this well." Don't let your confinement in the bottom of a well keep you from defining the world.

There is always a mountain taller than the one that you can see. Give up "needless" learning and put an end to your troubles. Practice *Tao* every day until you decrease your intelligence. Intelligence will not allow you to know *Tao* or God.

My Master, *Cheng Yu Li*, taught me how to become a humble, lovely dummy. By collecting and understanding the world and then detaching myself from that world, I became a lovely dummy. To become a lovely dummy is to gain access to the sacred gate of mysticism. A wise man often appears like a fool. Do not try to become too smart. Become that lovely dummy, so that you too may gain the key to the sacred gate of immortality.

Wisdom of *Tao* or Gad is not the intelligence. Wisdom of *Tao* facilitates intelligent actions, but intelligence is not *Tao*. Wisdom functions like intelligence; however, intelligence is not wisdom.

There should not be too much material "I." If "I" is too obvious you must learn to see the opposite of "I." Pause, through the stillness, to find out what is bleeding! What bleeding causes you to experience exorbitant amounts of the material "I?" Go beyond the superficial, material self to see and know the deeper spiritual self.

I have shared that you must learn to be more conscious of your own thought process. Once again, to do so, pretend that everyone can see your thoughts. Our thoughts can sometimes do just the opposite of what we express. Pretend that everyone can read your thoughts. Assume that everyone knows exactly what you think despite what you say. Most communication, my friend

is non-verbal; be totally conscious that people are reading those non-verbal words. Ask yourself, "Does it make me more responsible or fearful when I pretend that everyone can know my thoughts?" Be truthful to your spirit. By being conscious of your thoughts, you allow yourself to become a more extraordinary individual. You gain great mercy if you never have negative thoughts. No matter what someone says, choose to change the pattern of negative thought. The way you express yourself always exposes your true self. Only when you have a true "I" can you ready the organic "I." Only when you have the true organic "I" can you read the eyes of others. Choose not to repeat the mode of judging either yourself or others. Go beyond the model of judging. Be aware that agreeing and disagreeing are both forms of judging. Confirm someone's thoughts with passion, but in expressing your opinion, do not try to change a person's mind. There is no need to confirm, or to refute someone's opinion. If a spider bites me today, years later I do not grieve over the bite. So why lament over someone's opinion?

How many of us have a repeat pattern? Stop subconscious thought. When you don't feel comfortable, move your butt, do not pretend to be comfortable. However, acknowledge to yourself, "I am on training wheels." Allow yourself to fall. Have mercy when you do fall and show forgiveness. Forgive yourself and others. A soft tongue indicates heightened spiritual quality. You talk often in your head, repeating patterns again and again. Do something extraordinary. Stop repeating your patterns.

Results come from expectation. This is a two-sided story though. What kind of result from what kind of expectation?

Expectation comes as a doubled-edged sword. Are you ready to accept when you put out expectation? When you put out an expectation, do you attach a string to it? In doing so, you can drive yourself crazy.

Process: #1: Tell a silly joke or a funny story about yourself. In doing this process, learn to laugh at yourself. Laugh both externally and internally. A happy person is always able to fulfill the void in their heart by making fun of their self. When you make fun of yourself, without being deprecating or judgmental, you will heal yourself.

Process #2: Write a poem entitled "I."

Process: #3: Write a letter to the wounded "I." Write a one-page letter to "I."

Chapter 4

The Spiritual Self

For many reasons, my parents agreed to let me go to the temples of Wu Dang Mountain to cultivate my spiritual self. I was the only child in our family to leave home. My ma said to me, "Be good, learn and help others." Carrying that wisdom I set off with Kung Fu Master, *Guo Gao Yi*, crossing the country, sometimes hitchhiking, sometimes asking for donations, but most of the time just walking—over a thousand miles in all. Today it is a quick two-hour flight, but it took us over three months to travel to Wu Dang by foot. While we traveled, I was taught how to be a nice person, what virtue means, how to meditate to overcome my weakness, to overcome cold and heat, and how to survive without food. I learned how to be a beggar, to survive outdoors, and how to enjoy what we had. I think that this journey was one of the best things that I had ever done in my whole life; to travel by foot for over three months with my Master *Guo*, learning about life, humanity, the way of living, and learning to be close to nature and people. This journey prepared me to know my *Yuan* *Shen*, my original, spiritual self.

Yuan Shen is the original, sacred spirit that exists before, during and after what we regard as human life. *Yuan Shen* is on a journey in our body or human life. It is the guest to the hotel. It has no loyalty to the material self. Instead, it increases and decreases its sacred quality and power based upon the quality of the material self. The *Yuan Shen* in ninety-nine point nine, nine, nine, nine percent of the population comes from reincarnation. Only one in a million *Yuan Shen* comes from the world of immortals. In an ordinary human's life, you maintain the best quality of *Yuan Shen* by nurturing bodily essence (*Jing*) and vapor energy (*Qi*). By doing so, you balance your health and heal disease; you improve the quality of living and lengthen your life. The *Yuan Shen* determines the quality and the destination of a human being. Most people have a spiritual self that is crying for help. Understand this *Taoist* philosophy and you can reestablish lost connections to the sacred world. Through secret alchemical cultivation techniques of meditation, and purposeful living without attachment, you will find a way to go beyond normal human reincarnation and into the immortal world of your Master Within.

Many people think that spirituality is equivalent to doing yoga, eating vegetables, and wearing a cloak of spirituality. But that is not it! You can eat all the omega fatty acids you like, stand on your head, twist your legs into a full lotus, give to the beggar a morsel to eat, or help an old woman to cross the busy street; and this, I tell you, will not necessarily lead you to the profound happiness of knowing your spiritual self. Living in accordance with your true spiritual essence is what leads you to the true virtue and the spirituality of the Master Within. Deep down at the bottom of your heart, you know the true purpose of your life, the purpose that will lead you to spirituality and true happiness.

Allow your spirit to act like a spirit. It's okay to occasionally lose control a little bit. Sometimes that is what your spirit craves. Sometimes that is what your spirit needs. When your spirit is finally awakened, it may come to light in many ways. You may feel a unity, a total-stillness moment, the body may feel lost; sometimes there is a voice heard inside of you; and more. When the spiritual self is awakened, do not struggle and pull back to the self of intelligence or *Shi Shen*. Allow the original spirit to just be. Spirit needs that moment for temporary recharge. When the spiritual self-awakens sometimes it can do something very extraordinary. Your spirit projects out to show the path. R2D2, in the movie "Star Wars," spoke a language that only C3PO understood. If your spiritual self uses a language that logical, intelligent self does not understand, or an illogical picture shows up, or you experience strange feelings come on, or there is a voice, perhaps then intuition will follow and at that moment you must be willing to let go of your identity as a human. The spirit must function without form, and in illogical ways. There is a boundary you must cross over in order to get to the understanding of spiritual self.

MASTER CHEN

You must get in touch with your spiritual self. Learn to pretend that the solid "I" becomes the invisible "I." Pretend that your logical environment becomes illogical. The spiritual self is always able to access you, but your intelligent self isn't allowing you to merge with spirit. There is a tendency to block spirit and to not listen to spirit. Your world must go beyond the reality as you see it today. You become an active partner with the spiritual self rather than passive. Right now you are passive receiver. As you move in the other, illogical direction you become an active receiver. Because you are willing to let go of the borders that you have previously set for yourself and to gain access into the other unknown spiritual area, you then can access the hidden dragon and access the "illogical" function. You can actively access the illogical spiritual world. Do this and you are the one to ride the dragon. You can hear, sense, taste, and experience the power and the joy of the spirit. Don't step aside. When the opportunity presents itself, merge into it. You lose control of the self but still there is an awareness of self. Speaking of the merge or using logic doesn't work. Initially the union of spiritual self and material self is a passive experience, but later you become active as a facilitator. A sure way to stop the spiritual self from manifesting is to put up a wall of ego, emotion or illness. To allow the spiritual self to come in, you must clear your emotions and take out the garbage. Create an environment that supports the welcoming of the spiritual self.

Wisdom is not free. You earn wisdom through practice. In this modern age, many people have a misunderstanding of what spirituality is. These people associate themselves with something and then think they are spiritual. Be willing to bring something to the teacher, be it payment, determined labor, a committed heart or a full self. The teacher's journey has taken years full of disciplined work. Do not flatter your ego by thinking that association is spirituality.

Your spirit records your thoughts. Be responsible only to your own spirit. It is a "spirit crime" to put people in an unfair position and demand of that person, therein holding them accountable to your trust. It's very easy at any time to throw in the towel. If you sense that something is arises out of your expectations, don't throw the towel in. Don't waste your energy on pathetic thinking! Take action. Take the attitude that, "You can always wait for me." It is a spiritual disease to not respect the spirit. You have your own *Qi* doctor inside of you, so make change without further excuse. A pathetic attitude is like being a stone in the outhouse! Use your spirit to observe your words and your actions. How many times must you hear yourself talk without taking action? So many of us forever project thoughts without hearing them.

Chapter 5

Spiritual Wealth

Always know your goals and your limits in achieving them. (Always dream further than you can logically believe.) *Tao* rewards the challenge. When you live these principles you will always manifest what you want. Maintain the belief that, "I am going to do what it takes to get what I want." Ask yourself, "Am I the one to receive Gods gold?" If the answer is yes, then you will never need to be ashamed of being rich. Believe that you will be supported. When everything is ready, nature will follow and the people will come. God sends the right energy to you and money will flow. When you are the right one, money will drop from the sky. So the only question to ask is, "Am I the right one?" Be careful of how you project your thoughts. Only when you really have the right attitude about wealth will you be the right one to receive it. Then the prosperity will really flow in. It is your attitude that keeps you in the mud. You only hear the devil's voice. If you honestly ask yourself why, the answer is, because you made that choice.

Adjust your thoughts and actions. You are both a giver and receiver. Physically give charity and prosperity. Every dollar given without expectation of return is a virtuous exchange, the *Qi* or energy of *Tao*. You must learn to transfer the energy of *Tao*. Be a great facilitator of the dollar. If your attitude and energy do not flow smoothly, then both energies won't flow. Make sure you are a great facilitator, spending and exchanging. Do not possess with the attitude that, "I can't afford to give, I don't wish to give." Harboring hunger for money will only cause you to lose it. Be a huge wealth container! You have to keep pure and sacred. If the heart turns sour so will your wealth. Money is like a dragon that no one can possess. God or *Tao* knows who processes money well and who has the better attitude. If you don't confirm the gift with your heart, then the money doesn't stay. When you don't practice what you talk, then when the bridge crashes you won't be able to transfer the wealth to the other side. Be a high-quality bridge. Knowing that enough is enough brings the greatest happiness. If you stop the flow of the dollar, then the dollar doesn't flow. Acknowledge the principle of gift-giving. Give to someone who can't afford. Honor living your principle, then you can't be polluted.

A poor mentality is always poor, whereas, a rich mentality

remains rich. How many people are afraid that there is never enough? Dream bigger! Don't set yourself up for being poor. Don't predispose yourself to not be rich. When your spirit is poor your material self is poor. When you allow yourself to be spiritual, truly spiritual, then God will deliver the gold to your doorstep. Don't limit the size of your wealth. Wealth includes spiritual and material. Don't limit your wealth. Your mentality affects the outcome of your wealth. There is always enough gold for those who are the right ones to receive it.

Chapter 6

The Relationship Between *Yuan Shen* and *Shi Shen*

On our journey from the city of my birth to the temples of Wu Dang Mountain, we occasionally slept in run down temples. Other times we slept outdoors, sometimes under a roof and sometimes just right on the mountain, or right on the hillside. At times we received acts of kindness and were invited into somebody's house. We would take a corner to lie down in, or we would gather grass and straw to make a bed to rest upon. We never worried about what to eat. We trusted that there would be food available from nature or from people who would give it to us. Sometimes we simply didn't have food, so we would not eat for a day or two. This was during the Cultural Revolution in China, when many people were starving. If we had nothing to eat, we occasionally would eat grass roots, or we'd pick wild fruit and vegetables. We may not have eaten much, but people were kind and they shared their soup or their sweet potatoes as we traveled through towns. Our shoes would break and we'd have bruises and calluses all over our feet, but I never felt bad or worried because my teacher was strict and kind at the same time, teaching me and encouraging me. I felt secure. We traveled like this for over three months and it was fun! I was young, so my intelligent spirit had not come to rule my original, childlike spirit. This allowed me to be free and have fun because my mind had not learned to fear the unknown.

The *Yuan Shen* or original spirit does not recognize time or place. The *Shi Shen* is intelligent spirit. At the beginning of human life there is no existence of a *Shi Shen* or intelligent self. As humans learn the access to the material world, this gives birth to the *Shi Shen*. Humans are evolved from the innocence of a newborn baby, to the intelligence of youth and on to the wisdom of the peak power of the *Shi Shen*. At the same time *Shi Shen* is evolving, in most people *Yuan Shen* starts from a birth of mysterious capabilities and evolves towards numbness or unawareness of its true ability. *Yuan Shen* and *Shi Shen* are like master and servant, living in the same room with their position and power changing all the time. The wise man learns to be a dummy and the intelligent man fights for an empty statue of "self."

Sometimes *Shi Shen* says things that conflict with the *Yuan Shen*. The mind conflicts with the original spirit. The *Yuan Shen*, however, never gives up on the pursuit for purity. The original spirit is kindness, which we never give up, but *Shi Shen* sometimes contradicts this original spirit. The *Shi Shen* may not allow the *Yuan Shen* to speak or act freely. We must learn to live and let live! Live and let live is equal to unconditional love. Once you are able to love unconditionally, then you will break from the cycle of living in expectation of others. Learn to forgive yourself of being a victim. Only then can you overpower your pains and aches. Stupid people look for perfection in themselves, others, and the world. Life is not perfect! If you always try to defend yourself for being a victim, then you are already a victim again. There is no need to defend your self. Give up the desire to "win." Give up the fear of death. There is no need for offense or defense. Life is merely a puzzle. Welcome your opportunity to solve this puzzle. Always look for the other side, the dialectic side of "me." If you can know one side of "me," then you can know the other side of "me." Strive to understand the opposite of what you are feeling. However, always be consistent with what you believe. Walk the Talk! What you believe can change, but until then, walk the talk for what you believe today! Do not blame and become a victim.

At the start of our cross-country journey to the temple, I had a few early nights of regret but during the daytime I always said, "I'll be okay. I'll be fine." The desire to learn overcame my fear. I trusted that I would be brought to a magical place, a mystical mountain to meet a spiritual master who had chosen me to learn ancient wisdom. I would learn Kung Fu from this mystical old man. That desire and that motivation kept me going. We traveled three months to arrive at Wu Dang Mountain.

You must follow your head, heart and gut. The root of knowing comes from the gut. This is where instinct is born, in the *Dan Tian*, located about an inch below the navel. This is the furnace where *Jing* and *Qi* are purified to be transmuted to *Shen*. In China they say that we become stupid because at birth we are cut off at the gut, our umbilical cord is cut there. In today's world, our external environment influences us too much, and as a result, we work only from our head and heart. You need to go deeper, to your original condition, your *Xing* or essential nature. You need to find your eternal life or *Ming*. You were in the past one with eternal life. Separation came with the separation of *Xing* and *Ming*. Separation from eternal life makes us a slave of our emotions. Vulnerability is created from this separation.

Right now, your Master Within is your intelligence. This is a fake master. You need to find the original, true dragon, merge the black and the white of *Yin* and *Yang* to find the mystical dragon. This comes from the pre-heaven stage before your birth mother and father merged. The true dragon has to come from the *Yuan Shen*, from the original spirit. This is the dragon that creates your life. Before birth, you spend nine months in darkness and stillness to nurture your true spirit. Then birth happens.

Chapter 7

Follow Nature to Death and
Reverse Nature to Immortality

I remember the first day I walked into the small, rundown and broken temple.   I saw an elderly woman dressed as a priestess with a funny hat, the primordial hat and a blue robe, a finely embroidered blue robe.   She was sitting there waiting for me.   She said to me, "I hear you're coming from far away.   I knew you were arriving today. I have been waiting for you for so long." I replied, "Master, master, why do you wait for me?" She said, "You are the right one to learn my tradition. You are the one who is going to carry my tradition. From today on, you are my son. You are under my care to study. It will be very hard work, so I expect you to be disciplined to learn."

I was only six years old, and to me, this master looked very kind. At the time, she was one hundred years old, but she had a bright face, appearing very young with a bright red aura, and two kind but serious eyes that were full of love. She was sitting very upright and she gave me her blessing. I was very moved. I knelt down and in tears I said, "Okay teach me what I have to do. I'm not afraid to be disciplined. I'm not afraid to work hard. Just show me what I have to do. Just tell me what I need to do to deserve to learn." My Master laughed and smiled and said, "Okay, that is the kind of person I want to teach."

Those were my early years. The time I grew up in my home village was not easy. During the early years, before age six, I was very poor but I learned a great deal from my mother. I learned to persevere. I was never proud that I was famous for my skills. I merely thought, "I'm a useful person, I'm happy that I can help people. I'm happy that I can relay a message, happy that I can make people feel good." I was taught by one of the few female Taoist priests, learning about kindness, virtue and how to live humbly. This early life was an interesting life.

In life's journey, birth, growth, aging and death are the ordinary human being's nature. We are born with innocence, grow with many struggles, age with stress, and finally we die with regret and helplessness. Ordinary humans do not have control over their life's destiny. They continually fall into the cycle of reincarnation from one life journey to another. When we learn the secret cultivation techniques to reverse aging and increase the quality of life, we will follow birth to growing with virtue and happiness and continue growing to immortality. Cultivating immortality reverses the destiny of human nature. We have the power to design our own human life. By designing where, how, and when to live, you are the true master of the self. My Master lived to one hundred and thirty years old. She was living proof of great human longevity. My Master *Li's* story is a living proof of human immortality.

Your mission in life is to find the tools and merge these tools with wisdom to break open heaven's door, returning void to Tao. To grow into heaven, you need the human body to walk you to the gate so that the spirit can then merge in. The physical body is not the perfect vehicle to get you to the gate. Returning to the gate is the motion of Tao. To do so, you practice reversal. You are reversing your thinking and life to become as a baby and return to Tao.

In mandarin Chinese, *"Nei Shi,"* means "Look internally," and *"Jing Zuo"* means "Sitting still." You combine the two, sitting still or meditating to look internally. *"Tu Na,"* means "Breathe in and breathe out." *"Tiao Xi"* means "Regulate your breath." Breathe in and breathe out while regulating your breath. By sitting still and looking internally while regulating the breath, you reverse the nature of human existence.

Reversing the nature of human existence also pertains to everyday life. Whenever you take a side on an issue, without being aware of it, you are already in trouble. You have already blocked the flow of original spirit. Look dialectically to see both sides of an issue. Emit *Qi* to dissolve blocks, germs, and viruses. Balance the germ and it vanishes. Balance the argument and it vanishes. You must have a passion for solving the puzzle to balance and return to *Tao*. Balance and vanish! Don't get hung up on results. Before you take action, be still and listen to your body. Look inside! When you return to the stillness and become quiet, often times an issue disperses. Do not label things; it is merely *Tao* giving you the opportunity for internal reflection.

The Bible describes these concepts in an encrypted form. The first chapter in the Bible and the first chapter in *Tao Te Ching* say one and the same thing: *Yang* to *Yin* and *Yin* to *Yang*. Following nature brings you to death; reversing nature brings you to immortality. Following human nature removes you from the Garden of Eden.

The snake in the garden is the divide between white and black!

The snake separates the *Yin* from the *Yang*. The snake is the boundary! You must cross that boundary to reach immortality. The snake is the third side of the coin. It represents the post-heaven dragon. The snake represents human sexual energy. Sexual energy fosters the difference between mortality and immortality. Use it wisely to become immortal. Use it indiscriminately to become a mere human.

PART II

Why Am I Here?

Chapter 8

Harmony Between Man and God

Are we here to redeem a deed or repay a debt? Or are we here simply to live and find the way to free ourselves from reincarnation? By understanding the question, "Who am I?" you can then go back to answer the question of "Why am I here?" Human intelligence continuously increases throughout the human world of development.

As human scientific development advances, human intelligence increases, but our recognition of the world is beyond the human limit. As a result, the primordial relationship between man and heaven has been broken. People united with heaven as one is the most important belief in Taoism. So harmony between man and God, the trust between man and God, is at its greatest crisis. When the world changed from an original, traditional world where people worked closely with the land and nature, to a modern, industrial world where capitalism and modern science have continually developed, the human interior cosmos and harmonious relationship was dramatically damaged. At the same time, the relationship between mankind and the exterior cosmos also faces increased crisis. *Tao* follows what is nature. Regardless of what mankind accumulates or accomplishes to give back to human life, the quality of our cosmos is affected. The continuous reincarnation of mankind is based, in part, on worldly change and our resultant attachment to this worldly "accomplishment." We can explain, "Why am I here?" by reviewing the concept of Taoist reincarnation, first to clarify where we come from, and then to explain where we are going.

This crisis that exists between man and God also affects people who have spirituality. It affects the people who have come to enlighten all humans so that they can break through the limitations of the material world and evolve closer to spiritual world. These spiritual people have a much tougher task at hand.

Regardless the challenge, you can build up credits and break through *Tao* by cultivating your essential nature or *Xing*. You cultivate internal light to ultimately fix the quality of the human physical body. You cultivate the best human physical body quality so as to carry the best spirituality; then there is unity between your spirit and the body. This enables you to achieve the ability to cultivate immortality, eventually enabling you to return to your home, freeing you from the cycle of reincarnation.

If you are unable to achieve immortality in this lifetime, then whatever accomplishment is made in this lifetime will lead you to a better reincarnation in your next lifetime. The reason you, as a human, are in this world is to continue to improve the quality of your present life, leading you to an improvement of your next reincarnation, eventually leading you to the breakthrough of continued reincarnation and finding your way home. That is the reason you have come here to this earth. Once you understand, "Who am I?" and understand, "Why am I here?" then you are able to glean the question in the next chapter which is, "Where is my home?"   First, you must understand the human secret of "Why am I here?"

Process # 4: Write a page entitled "Who am I? Why am I here? Where am I going? How am I going to get to where I want to go?"

While doing the above process, ask yourself, "Why do I feel intimidated, and why do I give the power to be intimidated?" Life's purpose is to process happiness!   You already have happiness. Learn how to process it. You need to come to a state of balance, or *Zhong He*, center balance. By knowing yourself and knowing others, then you will never lose one battle!   Know yourself! The ego can blind conscience and wisdom. Let go of ego, let go of fear and death. Learn how to be entertained in this challenge. Passionately learn about intimidation. See and don't see, remain completely detached from what it is that you see. A baby does not know the difference or understand the concept of good and bad, or clean and dirty. You, too, must give up these preconceived concepts as they limit your scope to fully see and understand. Learn to turn mud into energy!

Process # 5: Identify the three emotions that you deal with most often.

Process # 6: Identify three hopes that you wish to accomplish in life!

Chapter 9

The Taoist Concept of Reincarnation

Training at the temple was very hard. In the summertime, we had to get up about four o'clock in the morning to start training, meditate, sweep the temple, and gather wood chips and tree branches for the cooking fire. We got up early enough to beat the rooster's crow. When in training, you must be up early to do meditation, to rise with the sun, to rise with the *Qi*, with the energy of the universe. You get up early and are not lazy. For a child, it is a little hard to get up at first, but if you get a bit of a whip on the butt, to get you up the first few times, then slowly you get into a routine.

A person comes to this world or is born through the merger of the *Yin* and *Yang* energy. From thousands of years before, to thousands of years later you are the same spirit merely in different forms. Males and females take their same spirit with different forms and different life journeys.

We live in this world to have a happy journey. There is no heaven or hell. We just live and find a way to balance between body, mind and spirit. Find a way to reconnect with the cosmos. Once we balance and harmonize body and spirit, we are able to live a happy, healthy and long life. For that reason, there is no debt to pay from past lives, and there is no stress of how to live the next life. All that exists is now! All concerns will be solved without attachment to fear and desire of the past and future. Based upon a harmonious and happy longevity, people are capable of living beyond the ordinary human nature. People are also able to connect with the immortal world that we call home.

In the Taoist concept of reincarnation, everyone is here to find a way to go home. You might ask, "Why do we separate from heaven only to return?" The origin of your ancestors, the origin of each *Jing* lineage, back to the original lineage, comes from the immortal world. In the beginning of your lineage, there was a male immortal and female immortal with *Yin* within *Yang*. These immortals, like humans, developed a desire or affinity. That is, they had love emotions toward each other. When immortals have a human desire, they automatically get *Yang Shen* of supreme spirit, which is supposed to make them immortal, but the supreme spirit is downgraded to the earth. So, from the immortal world of *Yang*, they drop down into the *Yin Yang* world here on earth. Earth is the *Yin Yang* world. It is a spring spirit that comes down. The male immortal is *Yang Shen* or *Yang* original spirit and the female immortal is *Yin* original spirit. Both come down to earth and fall in love with each other. Man and woman immortal become man and woman human when the man and woman immortal unite together to give birth. The male immortal becomes man on earth and female immortal becomes female on earth. They bring this affinity for each other from the universe, from the immortal world. So they have to look for each other to form a pair. This is what we call soul mates. Although they find the soul mate union, the union that is constructing the *Yin* and *Yang* unity is a post-heaven unity. The saying goes, "*Wuji* to *Taiji*," stillness to movement. The Immortal was *Wuji*, without any thought or desire. *Wuji* was an immortal that followed a love affinity and became *Taiji*. *Taiji* created two forms, *Yin* and *Yang*. When the immortals developed this affinity for love and feeling for each other, they had *Yin* and *Yang* and automatically materialized on earth, becoming man and woman. This is called *Liang Yi*, creating four forms: greater *Yin* and lesser *Yin*, greater *Yang* and lesser *Yang*. When *Yin* and *Yang* get together to form a relationship, man and woman marry and give birth to man and woman again. This is where creating ten thousand people comes from. Man is attracted to woman and they give birth to man and woman. When woman is attracted to man they also give birth to female and male. The lineage continues to cross and link through infinity of lineages, for hundreds of generations. Your generation came from this same source. You are now just continuing to reincarnate. The immortal spirit, *Yang Shen,* came first from the immortal world, and then into the human world, finally becoming the world of *Yin Yang*. *Yang Shen* or original spirit have no concept of time and space so they continually reincarnate. Time is only judged by man's intelligence. Time is not a concept of original spirit; therefore the original spirit just keeps coming, in different forms, into the human body. To stop the cycle of reincarnation, you must stop the desire and return to stillness. Stillness is the root of Tao.

Everybody's original spirit is tied to his or her own lineage. The female is tied to her maternal lineage and the male to his paternal lineage. For the male, the spirit comes back into every third, fifth, seventh and ninth generation, and for the female it is every second, forth, sixth, and eighth generation. Parents are windows for their children. One spirit creates thousands of forms. You are facilitator and creator. For one spirit there are three hundred and sixty forms all simultaneously processing. Any of these can come out in any form in any relationship to you. How can you earn enough credit that one day the three hundred and sixty all become one? How can you stop the whole incarnation process?

You are all here for a reason. That reason is to merge as one, to stop the process of reincarnation. You incarnate to find balance and harmony. Each form needs its own time to learn. We are all in different places because we are stuck with our influences, with the logic of our time while incarnated. Know that immortals have desires too, temptations as well. We are all looking to reunite with God. Learn to be human, and then you can merge again. Understand the concept that "It just it!" It is a huge responsibility to live in this life. You carry the whole mission; you carry your whole lineage. Learn how to see and not see, knowing and not knowing. Learn how you take one concept and let go of another. Take the logic and then destroy it to take on a new one. It's your choice. We all have our own journey, but the purpose is the same.

Being caught between the worlds leaves us slaves to the material world. We all have experiences in this incarnation to be free. It takes just one person's logic to go beyond comfort, beyond temptation, beyond desire. It just takes one. This one is you.

You are here to integrate every level of energy. Each life journey affects seven generations, three generations behind, three generation ahead and this present generation. Take upon yourself the responsibility to awaken. Your practice influences the seven generations, so doing your practice helps to influence your ultimate purpose.

There are thirty-six heavens. Some immortals need to come back to complete a mission as part of their cultivation. Each immortal also has its journey. If they fall into temptation, then they get trapped again! Immortals can make mistakes, but the darkness can have enlightenment! There is no absolute. It is dialectical.

The reason you are here is to stop this cycle of reincarnation. Without stopping the cycle of reincarnation you will continuously fall into the world of *Yin* and the world of the *Yin/Yang*. You will continually recycle until one day one person in your lineage breaks through, understanding this common affinity. For this reason, you become enlightened to stop desire, stop entertaining life, stop looking for things. In place of this, you focus on cultivating essential nature, cultivating your virtue and then improving the quality of the physical body by stopping abuse of the material life. Spiritual life and material life are then completely reunited. Each individual man finishes his own reincarnation. Each woman finishes her own reincarnation, and both return to the immortal world of *Yang* and exist in the immortal world rather than in the world of *Yin* and the world of *Yin* and *Yang*.

As long as you look, you do not see, but as soon as you see, then there is no more looking. Break through, break through *Tao* and build up the credit in order to see. You enter the human world to have an opportunity to cultivate the eternal life of the physical body, along with cultivating virtue. Then, you can break through to get out of world. Getting out of the world is to return to the eternal existence of the immortal world. Short of that, you will reincarnate. Not until you understand why you are here will you gain the motivation to move on.

Enjoy the lotus and respect the mud. Your human, material life is like mud. Mud contributes to the nutrition of the lotus giving both the flower and the mud beauty. An immortal is the lotus, but you have to live in the muddy life of the human before you can become immortal. There is another reason as to why you are here. You come to the earth to experience life. It is in experiencing life that you get an opportunity to train and cultivate the physical body to the extreme condition that gives you the key for immortality. You come to this material life to understand the stress, to understand the desire, and to understand the meaning of this material life. Through understanding, you can break through and become the sage. This gives you the platform for cultivating immortality. This is the reason why you are here. You have to first taste bitterness before you can know sweetness.

The Bible also tells the story of "Why am I here?" Adam and Eve initially did not have the intelligent spirit, or the *Shi Shen*, but the snake influenced them to have desire and therefore, God evicted them from paradise, the world of *Yang*, telling them that now they must become as ordinary man and woman. They then conceived and had a family. This cycle will continue until we come to understand our relationship with God. The reason you are in the world is to cultivate each other and unite each other to come close to God one more time and then, to go back to heaven.

"Learn to turn Mud into energy."

Bravery =7
"Altruism is the ultimate form of selfishness."

Chapter 10

Build Up the Credit and Break Through Tao

In the early morning, we would arise at four o'clock to start our physical workout. We stretched, meditated, and finally did the major work, like sweeping the temple, and lighting incense. I cared for my Master; she was my mother. It is a tradition to care for your master—washing clothes and cooking for your master every morning on top of the normal routine of stretching, exercising, meditation, and burning incense.

Thru the wintertime we rose one hour later at five o'clock, with the rooster. Winters were extremely cold. We didn't have heat like most people have now. This was the countryside and we lived in ancient temples. Our temple was run down, half destroyed by the Red Guard. It was destroyed because this was the time of the Cultural Revolution. The whole mountain only had twenty-five priests left. During earlier, stronger times, in the nineteen twenties, thirties and the early forties, we had hundreds of priests on the mountains. They were highly skilled priests. But during the Cultural Revolution, many priests were tortured to death, or were forced to go back to the communities. Temples and statues were destroyed. Artifacts were taken away. Red Guard took the Taoist priests to be "re-educated." It was called re-education, but in reality they were sent to labor camps, sent down to the villages to learn from farmers, that kind of Cultural Revolution activity. So we didn't have many people left, mostly they were the very old who had no family or who had been raised in the temple. A few priests were allowed to remain because local farmers and village people protected them. Local pilgrims protected them and supported them with food. But they were mostly very old.

At that time, my Master *Li* was already one hundred years old. When I came, I had to pretend that I was adopted and that I was an orphan, an abandoned boy with no parents. My Master took me in by mercy and I served her and took care of her. Since I cleaned and took care of her life, the Red Guard allowed me to stay. My Master practiced for over eighty years in the temple, so she was well known by the local people. She was such a reputable person, such a famous person, so the people protected her. When the Red Guard came to destroy her, local people came to her protection and wouldn't let them take her to torture her.

So in the wintertime we were very cold, the temple was broken and snow flew in freely. We tried to keep one corner of the room warm by using straw to block the wind from coming in and burning wood chips in a little burner. Winters were hard, but the training was amazing. The master trained in the snow, doing standing meditation in the snow with only a light jacket. We would wear just a thin cotton jacket while standing in the cold and learning to beat the cold using our internal energy. At the beginning of this training I got sick from the cold but with time, I learned to beat the cold through meditation, through stretching, through tai chi and Kung Fu movements. I learned how to beat the cold out of my body. This training in the cold was mostly about learning discipline and also learning techniques to withstand extreme elements.

You are here on earth to learn about conscience, mercy and forgiveness. Love yourself first before you love the world. In each life-journey we learn to be a more compassionate, loving and conscientious persons. Therefore, bring out the greatest credit of virtue in this life to free yourself from the past and future. Then, you will live a better and better life in one journey after the next. By doing so, you will eventually be guided to the right path for immortality. It is all based upon the quality and quantity of virtue. You will be guided to break through on your own. This differs from many religions where the reliance is upon a preacher. When you do thirty-six hundred good deeds, without claiming credit for those good deeds or carrying expectations for those deeds, then you will reach immortality.

I don't remember the exact year; maybe it was during the first or second year my time in Wu Dang, perhaps late 1972. I had been living at the temple for only a short while. Red Guards came to destroy the artifacts and statues. My Master was there. Two forty-year-old younger servants, who were also priests, had been chased away. But my master, who was one hundred years old, couldn't be chased away. They dragged her on the ground for over one hundred meters. Her back was raw and bleeding from being dragged. Each time they let her go, she merely turned and crawled back to the temple. She had that kind of dedication and devotion. I wanted to hate the guards but she told me, "This is just the nature of the universe. These young people, they don't know. Although they are aggressive, it is not their fault, it is the nature of life."

During the revolution, any religion was considered anti-Chinese Government. The government spread the word that any kind of illusional or mystical thinking was equal to committing a crime. Serving the spirit of God was a crime because communism didn't believe in God, it didn't believe in anything spiritual. Nobody was allowed to believe in Buddha or in Tao, even though for the past three to four thousand years we had been doing just that. Anyone who served God was considered to be anti-government, anti-socialism and anti-communism.

Even though they dragged my Master, she was able to forgive them and say, "It is not these young people's fault. They just follow the nature of politics and society of the time. I just happened to be their target and I served their purpose." It broke my heart to see her dragged on the ground. My little heart was angry and full of revenge. I wished I could just bury them right there. My Master saw this and said, "Perhaps this is your first lesson to learn, a lesson about forgiveness and mercy, and to not hate and be aggressive with revenge for people who are hot in their head right now."

My Master used her own example to help me process mercy, compassion and forgiveness to people. After that incident, we often went to a rural noodle factory. We hiked there. We would go to the gutter and to pick up scattered noodles. Then we would carry them up to the temple. We hiked around for hours. Behind the temple there is a spring where we washed the noodles. We then blessed the noodles and took them to people who were extremely poor and dying. My Master always showed compassion, even when we went hungry ourselves. Part of learning humanity is to love people. We didn't hate the Red Guard for following their nature at that time. We didn't need to understand why; we just happened to be there. Who knows, maybe we were a lesson for these young people sometime in their future, when they woke up. Perhaps they would one day remember what they had done and grow from there. Maybe my Master being dragged on the ground happened to be my lesson to learn. My Master *Li* just provided herself as a lesson, as a teaching tool. She would say, "Every one of us in our life can be the teaching material. Just relax. Heaven and Earth love and understand everyone."

Tao has three treasures. Practice these three treasures and you can learn to embrace both weakness and goodness. The first treasure is conscience. To find conscience be who you are, be kind to yourself. You are a diamond in the mud. Maintain virtue and do not fear mud. A diamond in the mud is still a diamond. The second treasure is mercy. Mercy plays no games and carries no judgment. You must possess unlimited and unconditional love, unconditional mercy. The third treasure of *Tao* is forgiveness. Maintain the power and application and you are always able to provide forgiveness. You must kiss yourself rather than beat yourself up.

Taoist principle says, "Be open and share equally." A poor mentality is always poor! Possess nothing and take everything. You can't possess unless you share. To give is to receive, but you can't place expectations on your giving. You can't expect that if you give something you will receive something in return. If you truly want good results, you must first empty the bucket. If you are true to yourself, then any guilt will be removed. As a result, there will be no persecution or betrayal. Have faith in yourself. Do not lock the door before your rewards come. Be truthful to yourself and have faith in yourself. Find the courage to bring joy to your life.

To practice virtuous giving, you can form a group with perhaps twenty like-minded individuals. Unite this group as one by forming an entity for charity. Then, if each person gives ten dollars, it is as though each of the twenty people in the group has given a two hundred dollar charity donation. Ten dollars multiplied by the twenty people gives the two hundred dollar gift. In doing charity as a group, with everybody giving the same amount, ego is left behind. This type of giving will help to free you from twisted energy. When you know where your "charity" is going, then it is not charity. Too much energy and ego are attached. Give to a trusted person or fund anonymously and allow them to put the charity to good use.

The only way to receive is by giving. Appreciate life and appreciate God. If you become greedy, then you are not qualified to become a receiver of God. You must be willing to give everything away. Change life by learning how to give to charity. Do not have attachment to your giving. Do not look for rewards from your giving. There is value in your work. "Tao-uable," (valuable) was the first word that I learned when coming to the United States from China. All your contributions have value. Work the structure of success.

Cultivate virtue to understand *Tao*. Stillness is the most important tool for breaking through to *Tao*. Virtue is the mechanism for helping you to find stillness. This is not about being good to others. You are walking alone! This is about yourself. Your process needs attention. Things get tangled up if you don't work through and organize them. Yesterday's unorganized stuff becomes today's entanglements.

As a human, we create a clockwise spin to move forward but we forget to unwind. Check yourself at least three times a day to make sure that you give yourself the opportunity to unwind. Confucianism and Taoism sometimes follow the same path. Organize your thoughts, emotions and spiritual issues so that you do not sleep with pain or suffering. If you do not do so, your spirit will need to clean house when it finishes this journey. Everyone has different frequencies to organize. Checking your self will help to organize things. You live in the material world, so naturally there will be garbage. You will need a garbage disposal system. Collect the essence from the mud without collecting the mud. Find purity even in the negativity.

I ask you once again, "What is spirituality? What does it mean to be spiritual?" Spirituality is in living faithfully to your true essence. In your everyday life, what do you see? Do you see someone who acts spiritual, but doesn't seem to be so? What do you do? Do you practice what you preach, or is there an abuse of power? Ego-based pretending only gives but never receives. This is not genuine. Holding spirituality only when you do your practices, but then, when in the world going back to judgment, close-mindedness and rigidity in belief is not genuine spirituality. If you believe that only what you do is right, this is not genuine spirituality. This pretending cancels out all your spiritual practices. Un-virtuous gain for one penny only brings you closer to your coffin. True spirituality is twenty-four hours a day. Maintain the same conscience, the same mercy and the same forgiveness twenty-four hours a day, seven days a week, fifty-two weeks a year for your lifetime. That is spirituality.

At the beginning of my training, before I learned anything, I used human nature to fight off cold. Standing in the winter cold with only a light jacket, for up to two hours at a time, I became cold, near to frozen and would almost die. My lips turned blue, my ears froze. But I learned to obey and to listen to the master's instruction. We trained under cover, behind the temple and at night, or outside of the village. Because we trained secretly, we couldn't do just anything. We couldn't even talk, because it was so secret. It was so sacred. We fully understood that the Cultural Revolution was trying to destroy our tradition. Our Kung Fu was in danger, because there were no disciples to continue the tradition. That kind of duty and that kind of mission helped me to build discipline to stand, despite the freezing cold. Without the master saying, "Okay, you can go," I did not dare ask to stop. Initially, I just stayed with human nature and was cold. Later, because I was disciplined and satisfied my Kung Fu master, he passed me and then he started teaching me how to breathe and how to use my mind to beat the cold. Soon enough, I learned to have fun doing standing meditation for two hours while feeling heat engulf me as the snow melted around me. That was how we knew we actually learned the lesson. When I passed, I learned something good. And you know, I learned something good to know.

Control what enters the mind and soul. Since you have a logical mind, why not entertain it! However, use virtue as a filter. Use *Tao* as a filter. Ask yourself, "What serves my ultimate purpose, my ultimate purpose of ending the cycle of reincarnation?" If something does not serve this purpose, then simply put, delete it from your life. Sometimes you may use your intellectual mind; however, your spirit is not so conscious. Your spirit is affected in an illogical way. This can be more dangerous than consciously controlling what enters your mind. You must use your array of Taoist weapons to filter out what blocks your ultimate purpose. Don't hesitate to filter it out of your life. True Taoist priests live with the wisdom of the sword hanging over their head, so they never have to worry about thinking what to filter out.   Only those who pretend to be God need to worry about the sword. Ego-initiated virtue is not true virtue.

Always appreciate gifts. It is in giving that you and others have the motivation and original intent to make another person happy.   The dialectical of giving is receiving.   From the subconscious, it is something that you want. The gift is delivered from God, so make good use of it. If you can't make use of a gift, then donate or give it away with sincerity. Whatever action you take, you must have appreciation. Take the energy of the gift and make it multiply. If you don't notice little things, then why should God deliver again? If you can't appreciate, then gifts will pass you by, relationships will pass you by and life will pass you by.

Chapter 11

The Purpose of Getting into the World is for Getting Out of the World

I trained undercover at the temple for over ten years, from 1972 to 1982. My main teachers were Master *Li* and Master *Guo*. Master *Li* taught me ceremonial arts and metaphysical arts. She taught me the ceremonial Taoist arts of how to chant, how to do ceremonies and also, the most important thing she passed down was the tradition of alchemy. In our culture, we call it immortality training. It is the secret of immortality. Alchemy training traditionally is only done through oral teaching. It is only passed down secretly. Alchemy is the internal practice for getting out of the world.

For whatever reason, you get into the world for a happy journey, to learn about yourself and to learn about others. In doing so, you learn to guide your own spirit to return to the stillness of *Tao*. Cultivating stillness helps you to reach into the world of the void. You must not only learn to understand who you are, but also you must love and accept who you are. By achieving the wisdom of breaking through *Tao*, you evolve out of the material world and into the immortal world of living for an eternity, a life of joyful bliss.

Your ultimate purpose is to have a reunion of spirit and body to return home. Set the goal or the rat that you, as the cat, will play with. Make it fun and enjoyable. But your spirit must remember that this is not the ultimate goal. It is when you attach to an outcome that you will get reincarnated. You are seeking to end this cycle. Your goal needs to be that which serves your ultimate purpose of reunion. You know what this is. Listen to your gut. You know it when you hear it. When you set the goal to serve your own spirit, you will see that it serves others. Whereas, when you set the goal to serve others, you will lose all. When you know what your goal is, you must act immediately without hesitation. You can contemplate the question, "What if?" all day and for every day of your life. Continuous contemplation of, "What if?" is how opportunity slips away. Identify the goal and take action; otherwise you will set yourself up for failure right from the start.

Process # 7: Tomorrow be slightly, subtly different than today.

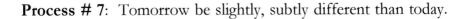

Do something that changes your spirit. Not a superficial change. This would mean nothing. Whatever external change you do, it must symbolize the spiritual change within.

It's in the fashion you project your spirit, how you present it. In this way you move from being ordinary to extraordinary. Be extraordinary always. Project your spirit. Don't let it be sloppy. We tend to believe in the illusion, "I should be." This is what we learn. Instead, you must project what you believe from the bottom of your heart. Until you project it, the spirit-world won't recognize it. Are you going to continue to misrepresent yourself, or will you be brave to project your real self? Are you going to continue to be a slave of life, or are you going to be a master? Will you continue to hide your true spirit, or will you let it out? Don't force yourself into a character you have nothing to do with. Even though it may be entertaining to others, it's not who you are. Project your true spirit, not a forgery!

The basic foundation for a goal is to gently start to understand who you really are. First though, you need an understanding of the world and the sacred Taoist view of reincarnation.

I was in training at the temple for ten years. For over eight of those years, Master *Li* put me to test. It took eight years for her to decide to teach me the immortality technique. She had to be absolutely certain that I was the right person. Even though she personally chose me, I had to be tested. She tested my wisdom, my discipline, my compassion, my knowledge, my heart and my virtue. Every single day was a test, to see if I was ready.

That was why every day, for eight years, we secretly studied Kung Fu and tai chi, and why Master *Guo* taught us *Qi Gong*.

Dian Tao is when everything has lost meaning, but now has the highest meaning and the highest purpose. *Dian* is to enlighten you into *Tao*. Usually, the master talks to you about this. When you understand this, your life changes, sometimes one-hundred-and-eighty degrees. True enlightenment comes from internal understanding. It's a harmonizing of frequencies. A voice comes to you and you are able to mimic it, to bounce back and forth with it. It's when both sides of you are on opposite sides of the universe, yet both can communicate with each other. Do they resonate? How long does this last? If you forget, the spirit again becomes a slave for others and for the world. Never forget. Understand that you have a giant "Master Within." Dance for yourself. Enjoy your own show. This is not serving others. Listen today to get that reflection and synchronicity and let it stay for the rest of your life-journey.

Understand this of what I speak today. When things beyond your control happen, will you allow it to take away the integrity of your understanding of your spirit? Will you truly stick with your life purpose and take life in a more entertaining way without deteriorating, or will you harm the quality of your spirit and fall deeper into reincarnation? Fall into the mud and emerge clean! The physical body may be dirty, but the spirit extracts the nutrients from the mud and becomes more powerful. You may not be able to understand the tragedies of life, but understand that every event is an entertaining event. Every event provides nutrients on the path to the gem. Respect the mud and enjoy the flower. The lotus extracts nutrition from the mud and is the

Book of JOB

most sacred flower on earth. The lotus symbolizes spirit; the mud symbolizes the physical body. "My life is so hard!" Okay, so what? Why not say, "My life is very rich!" I am so happy to have the challenge." Life can only contribute to your growth, not to your burden. The journey is about how to love and enjoy this life. Learn how to extract the nutrition from this life. Come out of this life a much wiser person.

The Art of War is in knowing yourself and knowing others. If you know yourself and others, you will never lose one battle. You will always win. Can you know yourself so well there is no sugar that can lure you away? When you know yourself so well, then there is not a single reason to continue dragging yourself back into reincarnation. Can you have that kind of determination? Do you have devotion to your life purpose; or like Adam and Eve, are you persuaded by the snake?

Many religions make it seem as though, "We are punished by God." They see all the disasters, all the hardships. We are tested again and again by God. When we read this with logic, we feel heavier and heavier. How could we ever reunite? We have so much we need to redeem. And we start to believe it. No! Look at it in a dialectical way and you can understand why God put us on this journey. God does love us. Lao Tsu taught about finding harmony in polarity. He interprets the true meaning of God. What is the meaning of life? How do we deal with a life as tragic as the Bible describes? Are we supposed to live in the fear many religions describe, or are we able to live with joy in the pain that they describe? How can you know sweetness without having tasted bitterness? How can you feel joy without having witnessed pain? In stillness there is no pain or joy. It just it! Can you dance with the devil or do you remain its slave? Can you live above your body? Identify body, identify spirit, merge and then go beyond. You are your own witness. You are your own cheerleader. Have mercy and love for yourself during every life event. Draw the wisdom, not the pain and shame from every life event.

Life is, absolutely, not about suffering. It may look like that, but when you turn it around, you see that every life event is an opportunity. It is nourishment for the spirit. Spirit can only grow through life events. <u>True enlightenment is not about fearing God, or the devil.</u>

I had many tests to pass. During ten years of training, I recall that the compassionate loving test was one of the hardest. The test was to gain knowledge about humanity, and then seeing what I had learned. Both of my masters gave me the assignment to be a true beggar on the street. I had to be a beggar, on my own, in the winter. I walked through three states on foot. The year was 1977 and the Cultural Revolution had just ended. The Revolution officially ended in 1976 when Chairman *Mao* passed away. China had just experienced its deepest human disaster in history. Every household experienced hunger, poverty, family betrayal and political assassinations. There was this unfathomable condition of mind that people were unable to escape. Everyone was literally a victim. Everyone distrusted each other. Children had sold their parents out, betraying them. Parents sold their children out, friends killed friends, friends sold friends out; students killed their teachers. Teachers had nowhere to teach. Knowledge was murdered. The people of China lived in a totally delusional world. Everyone lived the slogan, "Long live Chairman *Mao*, long live Chairman *Mao*." Everyone possessed a red book to feel associated with Chairman Mao. No one dared to be real. In that kind of political environment, can you imagine that I, at ten years old, tried to travel through three states? Can you imagine walking onto a doorstep and knocking on doors, knowing the family had no food, yet trying to beg for something to eat? Some families looked at me like an intruder; some families chased me with a dog; some children chased after me with rocks; other children chased me from the door with feces. It was in this setting that I learned about human weakness.

However, I also learned about human warmness and compassion. There were some people who took me in, feeding me and giving me warmth. When you experience this, you really, truly learn that humans have the greatest potential for compassion. At the end of this bitter journey, if there is only one thing that I learned, it was the merciful, compassionate capacity of human nature. This in itself brought great value to the whole journey. I love my Masters' teaching because it is so practical. It is so different from an ordinary person's thinking patterns.

The whole world can hate me, but that does not give me reason to hate the world. Why is that? Why should we not hate them back? When you hate the world, you hate yourself. Then you reincarnate. So, for your own selfish reason, love the world. The trap is, "If I'm hated, then I'm entitled to hate back." This, my friend, is playing a game with the devil. You have been drawn in without knowing it. This is the logic game. The devil is master of these games. You flounder with emotion. You confuse with judgment. Can you not play? If you have to play, can you play better than the devil?

How do you kill the devil? Love your enemy? No! This is a misstep of some religions. When God and the devil are sitting next to each other, how do you tell them apart? There is no answer. If there was, then you label which is devil and which is God. The cat can turn into the rat, and the rat can turn into the cat. This is the *Yin* and the *Yang*. When you tip to one extreme, you can turn it over; fifty-one percent changes the balance. It seems like a lot, but not if you take it one percent at a time. Even God has desires. Even God has the devil within.

In the reincarnation process, the percent of memory you come into is equal to the wisdom that you gather during each life incarnation. The more wisdom you gain, the better the next incarnation will be. Each life provides opportunity to collect wisdom to finish the journey. This life of yours has very good purpose.

You need to create a vehicle that produces the vibration and frequency with which to synchronize the spirit and the God. Five thousand year old Taoist wisdom has been passed from generation to generation teaching how to merge the Eternal Life Technique with the Essential Nature Practice. Without the proper practice to support you, the frequencies won't match. Simple prayer is somewhat of a meditative state, but alone, it will not allow you to reach synchronization. Taoism has a slogan, "My life is in my own hands, not in heaven's hands." What does this really mean? Taoism is practical. It has an actual process to practice in order to upgrade the human body, and to synchronize. The internal alchemy method enables you to really see your own spirit. You, as you create your immortality from within, awaken your immortality, and you see it right in front of you. Then, you can cross over and enter the *Yang* world.

Direct and indirect experiences shape us. Direct experience is from family lineage, the people we have contact with and self-studies. Indirect experience is the influence of the exterior: shows, books, movies, religions and community. Allow people to choose what resonates with them, what resonates with their heart and their intelligence. We all vibrate at different frequencies. Give freedom and give the possibility for others to find their own spirit by providing choice. Choice helps others to get home sooner, which is ultimately good for you.

Religion provides us a vehicle to carry our logic. Practice whatever it is. Change it when it needs to be changed. Even as an adult, remain free to choose what to believe. Any method you choose to use is a vehicle to carry the logic. Use what works to meet your own frequency. Religion is just the uniform. You are the vehicle and you are the driver. Be a human first. Find yourself and then you will become an extraordinary human. Take opportunities to remain free. Meditation is good. *Tai Chi* is good. Alchemy is even better. Alchemy is the greatest vehicle to see the merging with your own spirit. It is a scientific but illogical practice. You learn how to discover, nurture and then give birth to the immortal.

Process # 8: Write a poem entitled "I."

During the three months as a beggar, what kept me going

was my four years of training. By the age of ten I had already learned so much and my master had passed down a great deal of knowledge. I had great faith in what I learned and that is what kept me going. I knew that my Master without doubt believed that I was not dying. She had always told me that masters never put their disciple or student at risk. If they had not experienced it, then they would never put you through it. In the *Tao* this is called, "The head goes first," meaning that the master always knows—knows that I'm okay. With that firmly in mind, I went forward. It kept me going. That was one of the key tests to come back from.

You must be brave and see through your fear. Are you the entertainer of life, or is life entertaining you? What do you choose? Life doesn't abide by what you want. Entertain and look beyond. Look and live in both dimensions and then live in the third dimension. Live beyond the spiritual and material realms. Live in the place of the hidden dragon. You understand this when begging on your own for three months.

Your life show is dedicated to yourself, not for show to others. A mistake people often make is that, "Life is a stage and life is a play." Not so! This is like prostitution. You are asking for approval and expecting to get it. With this attitude you are just seeking to please. This is a big mistake. Life is not just you showing for others. It is a part of your own show for yourself. And you are in control of your show. Do you understand? You are the show. Do not prostitute yourself. Always learn to preserve your dignity and respect. Know who you are and what you want in your own life. Never downgrade. Life is not about survival. It is about how to find a way home. Be in the show to entertain yourself and not others. It's a lonely journey. It's a one-man show. If they don't cheer for you, it's only because they don't understand your show. So what? They are in your show. That's part of it. To get them to understand, you have to change everything; your posture, costume, script. Wrong! By compromising you delay your journey, sometimes even reroute your journey. You compromise your intelligence and your dignity. Once you lose it, you feel worthless. That is a sickness. You continue floating in that inner cycle and you are compromising your value. In the end, you actually compromise your journey. Your purpose for life is compromised and you become the biggest victim. You miss the end of the journey. You are searching for your own self. This is the journey. Why would you sacrifice so much just because you need to be somebody? In doing so, you give away your control. To become somebody, you sacrifice your integrity. Others can only give you an illusion of approval; an illusion of identity and you believe it to be real. I call this prostitution. You lose. You lose big time. You know where you are going. So no matter what is offered, and it might sound very sweet, very hopeful, or very valuable, you cannot give in. Once you bite the hook, you're done. Don't be a fish going for the bait; the hook is hidden. So, no matter what looks good, never, ever compromise your spirit. Never compromise your goal.

You absolutely need to set aim on the goal and never lose it. No matter what's out there, never let it hook you. Never bite it. It's a one-man show. Let the world cheer for you voluntarily. There is at least one person who will cheer for you and that will be you! You can select your own audience. Even if there are zero other people to cheer for you, you cheer for yourself. Do not look for people to cheer for you, lest you lose your integrity. Do not compromise your own integrity and your spirit. When you want something so badly, this is when you begin to compromise. But if you do something for dialectical reasons, you can entertain yourself, but be careful not to compromise your spirit. Be flexible, but this does not mean compromise. Flexible means, "Be more skillful, more logical." This just means you are a good actor or actress. Your purpose is to unite all generations and find your way home.

Your destiny is to find a way to unite with the spirit within you, to serve the immortal within. There are two of you, an inside and an outside. Sometimes their frequencies are different. Your true purpose is to merge the two to one. You need your own, marriage maker. It is about how to make the "snake" line dissolve into the void.

PART III

Where is My Home?

Chapter 12

What is the Destination?

Nearly everyone questions where they are from and where's their true home. Many religions have created a concept of heaven and hell. We teach people to find their sacred and spiritual home.

"Where is my home? After death where am I going?" For thousands of years these are some of the biggest fears of mankind. Man is not only afraid of living, but also, more afraid of dying. What is the destination of the death? Where are we going, what is the concept of the death? By explaining this concept, you are able to understand where your home is and where your destination is. In fact, you are in control of your own destination. You can affect the quality of your future. Do not live letting your purpose for living hang upon some preacher, or allow some master in the world to tell you where to go and how to go. Learn to turn to stillness, to look to the concept of the death. Then, you do not have any fear of confronting death. You laugh at it, rather than get heavy about death. Understand that the answer is in the home. When you have the map in your hand, you will never get lost. Absolutely do not listen to all the forceful preaching, all the forced preaching. We reveal three destinations of the world; the world of *Yin*, the world of *Yin* and *Yang*, and the world of *Yang*. We can explain who will go to which world and why we go to each of the three worlds. In the Taoist point of view it is very logical—the concept of the world and the concept of the life after.

Chapter 13

The World Beyond the Eyes

When I was eight years old, I also had a challenging test. One midnight, I was brought to a Chinese cemetery; it was not a luxurious cemetery like those found in this country. Here a little tomb, there a little tomb, the coffins were broken, the tombs crumbling down, skeletons hung out. At midnight, the cemetery crawled with ghosts—I just stood there. I could feel the ghosts and spirits around me. At eight years old I was without advanced learning. My master told me, "Okay, from midnight to three o'clock you walk through this cemetery." The cemetery was a half-mile long. There were hundreds of tombs and I was instructed to walk through it. I was so fearful that I cried and I was unable to move my feet. I was sensitive to spirits and very fearful. I couldn't do it, so my Master said, "Okay." I failed that first time. Though I failed that test, still my Master did not yell at me. Instead, she gave me a pat on my back and said, "It's okay. I too have failed in the past. I too failed with my Master. My Grand Master was also a female master," she said, "It's okay. Let's try again another time. Yes, there is a lot of energy there and it is very sad, but you know, you have to walk through with love. You have to walk without seeing them as a threat and you have to have compassion and love to do this." I learned and returned a month later, once again at midnight. This time I was able to say hello to every spirit and pass through without fear. It was a challenging test.

Taoism has the concept of the three worlds, the world of *Yin*, the world of *Yang* and the world of *Yin-Yang*. Based upon the quality of the *Yuan Shen* or eternal spirit, we can know that the majority of human spirits come from the world of *Yin*, which exists in a realm beyond our eyes. Spirits come from the *Yin* world and into the material *Yin-Yang* world of earth to take on various material forms, including that of a human. The original spirit serves as a guiding angel, so to speak, through one's life-journey. Regardless of whether it's happy, or not, the *Yuan Shen*; the original spirit resided in the world of *Yin* to wait for a new life process. Humans and all living forms take a life journey on the planet we call the *Yin-Yang* merged world (earth), the world that is the merging of *Yin* and *Yang* energy. Here the spirit and body can live in harmony or disharmony. The *Yin-Yang* world of earth serves as a bridge between the world of *Yin* and the world of *Yang*.

Yuan Shen in all living forms is cultivated to grand harmony through guiding instruction. Cultivating improves its quality, thereby breaking through the illusion of the *Yin-Yang* world to ultimately enter the world of the *Yang*—also located in a realm beyond our human eyes. The world of *Yang* is the world of immortals, whereas the world of *Yin* merely serves as a cultivating, nourishing and processing center for the departure and return of spirits to the *Yin-Yang* world of earth.

To repeat, in the Taoist point of view, there is the world of *Yin*, the world of *Yin-Yang* and the world of *Yang*. Ultimately, our original ancestors came from the world of the *Yang*. Human life is how we make our way back to the eternal home of *Yang*. Short of that return, we continue to live in the mud of the temporary world of the *Yin* and the *Yin-Yang*. Some religions call this the world of hell or purgatory, waiting to return to the material world of *Yin-Yang*. The destination is our choice— whether we stay in the earthly material world or return to the world of *Yang* our ultimate world

When I was fifteen years old I faced a martial arts test. It was rainy and the brook ran fast, causing flooding. On an ordinary day, you could see rocks above the surface and because of training you could run across these rocks pretty quickly. I could quickly touch on the rocks and jump over the brook. But on a flood day, the water was so high that it was not so easy. I couldn't use intelligence or memory to recall where the rocks were. I couldn't see the rocks and some had flushed away. Master *Guo* asked that I come to the brook and instructed, "Run through it." I stood there somewhat shocked. I replied, "I can't do it! Master I cannot do it. The water is so fast and cold." Master directed, "Just run." He was stricter than my master *Li* who could pat my back. He said, "You've got to run through it!"

So I conceded, "Okay, okay, I'll obey." So I ran and I fell into the water and was flushed down stream a hundred meters. Thinking back, I learned the lesson to trust your own ability and to trust your master's. Your master never puts you in danger. Your master never asks you to do what you are not capable of. Your Master sees ability that you have not been able to trust that you have. The second time through this test I just had fun. I jumped back and forth across the brook several times. It was about twenty to thirty feet across with no rocks visible. I just trusted that I could do it. I ran about fifteen feet on the shore. I felt weightless, very light, touching just the surface of the water, like flying. In ancient times we called this, "Flying *Qi Gong*." This technique uses the eight extraordinary channels and pre-heaven *Qi*. You must cleanse post-heaven energy so there is no garbage in your body, no blockages. You create access to internal energy to make your body weightless, allowing you to fly over. You already have the ability; it's just your mind that blocks it. Your mind sees the water. Your mind says, "No I cannot do it." I had to break through my mind to believe that I could do it and I had to say there is no water, "There is no such thing as water." All I saw was land and all I felt was flying through. I felt like there was no weight on me. Everyone has the capability to do flying *Qi Gong*. But you do have to go through training for a long time. It's a great amount of training with a highly skilled master to teach you internal alchemy, helping you to reach this skill level. I learned from this test to trust, to see nothing. Don't put concepts in your head to see blocks, just do things.

There are two energies, *Yin* and *Yang*, two kinds of dragons, white and black. A mystical dragon always creates ten thousand things. An emotion can be in ten thousand forms. Different forms can be manifested in different ways. However, ten thousand eventually return to the one. Hundreds of generations can be freed from one person's realization. One-person breaks through and all become one. Your whole lineage is only one dragon. Post-heaven spirit is a black dragon.

Chapter 14

Where Am I going?

The Cultural Revolution ended in the late 1970's. In 1982, although the revolution was over, people were still under its deep shadow and they were in fear of the government. There was a policy of no religious or ceremonial practice. Wu Dang Mountain was under a cloud of depression. There were no priests to come to the mountain and so from 1976 to 1982 there was no practice. We practiced in secret and were still in fear of the government. In 1982, the Chinese government changed policy to allow religious practice. The government took care of management and administration of the religions. They created the Taoist Association. My master told me, "It is the time for you to leave. If you stay at the Mountain, then all that you learned from me will be under government supervision, and you are not formally registered as a Taoist priest."

They required all Taoist priests to re-register. The first group of Taoists recorded from the community had to have background checks. They had to have a certain education and meet age requirements. I was only sixteen years old and in many of the demands I did not qualify. There was concern there would be no freedom to practice and there was a risk for exposure of my secret identity in the mountain. So my master said, "It's time for you to travel. Take what you have learned to the community. Do things for the community and verify your skill in the community. If you go away, you can preserve what you have learned. In time, you will return, return is the motion of the Tao." I knew, within, that one day I would return to the mountain. "For now, I will take what I have learned, practice and verify in life what I learned." Someday I would bring back to the Mountain what I learned from the community, teaching younger people and future generations.

Some people are afraid of both living and dying. In their life journey, they worry where it is they will go upon death. They continuously question why they are here and the purpose of life. When you understand the concept of three Taoist worlds, then you do not live in fear of death or live in the stress and pain of life. You understand that, to live or to die is just simply an illusion of human life. In truth, there is no end concept called death or beginning called birth. We introduce the existence of the three worlds so that everybody can understand the concept of afterlife as being just a continuation of earthly life, allowing you to make a choice of your own home. Based upon your level of cultivation, you will go to one of three homes.

Life and death are two sides of the same coin. You are still the same coin, the same spirit, just a different side. It's an illusion to see them as different. In reality we live in many different dimensions. Life is one journey continuing into the next journey. We hope the next journey is more beautiful. The highest journey is to become immortal, to return to your true home, the world of *Yang*. Where is your true home? This is found inside. It's the space inside. Most of us are defined by our emotions so the concept of home is very blurry. We have limited capacity to see. We get lost. We are lost sheep.

It may be pre-ordained as to when you are born and when you die, but through cultivation, you can get a "bonus" to live longer. When, where and how you will die can be changed. Destiny is changed with intention. We are allowed three opportunities to change and gain enlightenment in our life.

Chapter 15

Going to the World of Yin

Most of the human population suffers from the stresses of emotion and desire, decreasing the quantity and quality of bodily essence (*Jing*), vapor energy (*Qi*) and original spirit (*Shen*). This brings them to sickness and disease. Their life journey comes to an end bringing them back to the world of the *Yin*. Most people live life again and again to process the same stress. Journey after journey they return to the world of the *Yin* to process and be redeployed back into the world of *Yin* and *Yang* (earth). It is a journey without end.

Transformation takes time. There are eighteen floors of transformation in the world of *Yin*. Each floor can take ten or even one hundred years. In rare situations, you bring memories from previous lives. At each of the eighteen floors you remember the earth stage. When you get to the last floor you usually delete the memory. At the moment of death and the moment of birth, there can be no concept of living and dying. Ninety-nine, point nine percent of humans go through the earth and *Yin* world cycle many times.

If we get our original spirit (*Yuan Shen*) out of the head and into the *Dan Tian*, approximately two inches below the belly, then we have already changed our destiny. People and religions often use fear to dominate and control others. In Taoism, fear is not taught. *Tao* teaches happy living. Other approaches also do so, but with conditions. Insecurity and fear of the unknown lays the groundwork to be controlled. Your attitude on living and dying can change your next life. Live and have the best life that you can. "*Xiu Dao*," practice the *Tao*! *She Li*, are the pearls that consolidate from a cultivated person when they die. One Immortal serves one million people!

Chapter 16

Floating in the World of *Yin* and *Yang*

There is a certain population of humans who die with tragic trauma, accidents, sudden disease or suffer great emotional impact, such as people being murdered, or drowned. When they die they don't believe that they died. As a result, their spirits float outside of their bodies without immediate return to the world of the *Yin*. Their journey has not come to an end so their spirits float in between the world of the *Yin* and the *Yang*. We call this, temporary homelessness.

Chapter 17

Return to the World of the *Yang*

A very small percent of people live in grand harmony between spirit and body and in grand harmony between the spirit and the world beyond the eyes. They forever cultivate virtue and stillness. They practice internal alchemy techniques gaining access to the immortal world. Based upon the level of cultivation and achievement, they can be immortal on earth among people and immortal in heaven. This is the ultimate achievement. They finally find the true home, free from reincarnation, free from the material world, free to come and go as they choose. Some are free to choose any form, at any time and anywhere, without restriction between the three worlds.

The fundamental beginning of immortals came from the origin of the universe. The universe gave birth to original immortal *Yuan Shi* or original beginning—the highest God in Taoism. *Ling Bao* or Precious Treasure followed and then *Tao De, Tao* and Virtue—which is *Lao Tsu*. In the world of *Yang*, there are many different levels of accomplishment, whereas, in the *Yin* world, there is involuntary reincarnation. In the *Yang* world, there is complete choice and freedom around incarnation. Be human, be spirit. Be the best human, be the best spirit! "I am my own Master!"

Different patterns and frequencies carry different strengths. There are many frequencies animal, human and immortal. There are also many patterns, *Yin* channel, *Yang* channel and *Yin-Yang* channel. How do we know that we are not here in the past or the future? We travel with different frequencies and patterns through time and space. What do my dreams mean? How do I know that I am not in a dream? From the *Tao Te Ching* we know that one became two, two became three, three became ten thousand. In the one thousand years before and one thousand years after, how do you know it is not a different spirit? The physical form can be dispersed and the *Yuan Shen* or original spirit can travel. Immortality can change everything.

When we reincarnate, our pattern and frequency is passed to one of our descendents, for males it may go to the first, third or fifth generation, and for females, to the second, fourth, or sixth generation. Usually, it takes at least three generations to reincarnate; one or two is very rare. Usually, women reincarnate into their female lineage and men reincarnate into their male lineage. But sometimes a male and female can cross, male into female and female into male. Sometimes you accidentally cross over timelines.

There are "eighteen floors" in the *Yin* world. Ninety-nine point nine percent of humans will go to one of the 18 floors. Your level of virtue, determines what floor you go to. With higher cultivation you go to a higher floor in the world of *Yin*. Each floor carries different patterns. You process through each floor above until you have completed processing and are ready to be reincarnated.

Illness and blockage can create a gap between the original spirit (*Yuan Shen*) and the body. When the *Shen* unites with the body your senses turn in to the *Dan Tian*. The *Shen* goes into the body, so when the messenger comes to take you to the world of *Yin*, the messenger cannot see the *Yin Qi* between the body and *Shen*. You are then in the frequency of *Yang*. *Yang Shen* is when the body and original spirit are united. When you are a hundred percent connected to the *Yuan Shen* then you pass into the world of *Yang*. As a baby you are ninety percent connected to *Yuan Shen*. As a baby you are very connected to the original spirit, but not one hundred percent. As an adult this is reversed and you are perhaps only ten percent connected. Through cultivation of stillness you can reconnect to the *Yuan Shen* and not use your life credits. Then you can pass them to your immediate family or pass them in either direction for three generations, freeing seven generations from reincarnation.

PART IV

Happiness is the Choice of My Intent

Chapter 18

The Power of Will

Tao gives each human the gift of making choices. All living things have the ability to make choices. Make the choice of happiness over suffering and pain. To do so, you detach from current intelligence, let go of the intelligence that you have accumulated in your human life. By exercising the power of the will, you can strengthen the quality of your physical body. The choice of happiness is a matter of mind and intent. Once *Yuan Shen*, the original spirit gets strong, it enables you to have a better ability to make the choice of happiness.

After you understand the secret of "Who am I?" in chapter 1, "Why am I here?" in chapter 2 and "Where is my home?" in chapter 3, you grasp the secret of "I," the secret of the self. Once you understand the secret of the self, then choosing happiness is simply your personal choice, your wisdom choice. It's your intent already. A common affinity between you and the spiritual world causes you to make up your mind to choose the destination of your spiritual accomplishments and to choose the quality of present life. Understanding that intelligence is not equal to wisdom, each and every one of us has a common affinity with the immortal world. That you are reading this book means you have common affinity with your own destiny, with your immortal world. Inherently, this also means that you have the chance to become immortal in this lifetime. All you need to do is make up your mind to choose happiness. Use your wisdom to make your choice to be happy.

When you understand the secrets of "Who am I?" "Why am I here?" and "Where is my home?" it is your choice. You can choose happiness and immortality or alternatively, you can cultivate in the material human world and entertain suffering for life. Understand that making the wise choice is based upon the quality of your physical body and the quality of your spirit within. To make the choice of happiness, your good intention counts, but the choice is based more upon the quality of your original spirit (*Yuan Shen*). That quality can be improved through disciplined training of the body and through disciplined cultivation of your virtue. Disciplined cultivation will lead you to form the ability to make wise choices in moving towards immortality. However, just as my cultivation depended upon my learning from my master, so is your cultivation dependent upon learning ancient techniques from a capable master.

My journey to the West began when I left my Master *Li* and she gave to me one simple advice. "Everything will be ready, just wait for the wind to blow from the east." When the wind blows from the east, it meant that I would come to the West. That was her intimation. I thought, "In the Western world I have no relatives, I have no legal channel, to bring me to Western world." No family, no host, no people that I know. How do I get there? But I trusted my master, so I took that message seriously. In the mean time, I graduated from college and I was a teacher. Two Chinese brothers, from Stony Brook, Coram, Long Island, heard that their mother in Hong Kong suffered with bone cancer. The mother returned to her home in China to await her death. Both brothers came back to China to visit their mother. I was a high school teacher, but in my spare time I taught on the hill, under a pagoda by a garden. I was a well-known instructor, speaker and healer. The two brothers had distant relatives in my village and so, they heard about me. They traveled to my house, asking my parents if they would ask their son to diagnose and give treatment to the mother. My ma came and asked for me to come back to the countryside. She told me that she had promised the sons. I listened to my ma and went to the village to visit this old lady.

At first sight I see that the bad energy was not cancer. I told her, "This is not cancer. This is just bursitis in the shoulder." She was unable to lift her arm, bend her arm behind, dress herself, or care for herself at all. She was in huge pain and she had been misdiagnosed with cancer. She was of course depressed and dying. And when I said, "No! This is bursitis," she just lit up and said, "Really! Can you help?" I replied, "This is a piece of cake. I will do a few treatments and it is done. After about six treatments you should be healed." This was the first time I performed a healing in the countryside, on this old lady. She was about sixty years old, standing in the courtyard, just standing there and relaxing. I stood one meter away and emitted *Qi* to her. I pushed with both palms facing toward her, just like doing magic. The village people thought I was crazy, but they all knew I was mystical. Years later I still carried a reputation from when I was young and so they all just watched me, all the relatives along with a group of fifty or so people. Three feet away from the old lady, I pushed and pulled with my palms. While I did that the old lady started to dance. She started swinging and dancing wildly, involuntarily. The crowd murmured, "Oh no…. Did you just turn her into a witch? Is this dangerous?" But I had a pre-arranged agreement with both brothers—no matter what happened they were not allowed to come close. I continued walking around this lady emitting *Qi* and after the first treatment all her pain was gone. With two more treatments I was able to take the bursitis away and she has been fine, up until today, since 1990. It has been over twenty years now and she has been fine and happy. Because of this event I came to the United States.

At the time, it was illegal for immigration to the United

States. But this old lady said, "My two sons are from the U. S. You are going to the United States. This kind of skill has to go to the United States. It will make you rich. Let my sons pay for you to go. My sons will give you a loan of money with no interest. We'll give you the thirty thousand dollars. My two sons will take you." She ordered her two sons and of course they agreed to do it. Because it was illegal to immigrate to the United States at that time, they arranged, through illegal channels, to bring me. I was on a journey along with fifty-two other people to cross over.

Cultivating essential nature depends entirely on your individual choice to break through. Although cultivating life is also all based upon the authentic teaching of a master, the choice is for you as an individual to make. Taoist teachings are never kept secret for those who seek with great virtue. The teachings show people a way of cultivating body and spirit so that they have the ability to make the better choice, to go back home, reunite with God and return to the immortal world.

Happiness is the only purpose of life. Regardless of the circumstance, keep the happiness in your heart. Can you always remain faithful? Remaining faithful is how you can keep the joy in your heart. As soon as you don't have joy, you detour from your purpose and before long you are completely out of your journey.

Think about the distinctions between happy and not happy. Happiness encompasses two levels, one is material happiness and the other is spiritual happiness. In Taoism, the concept of happiness is more about the achievement of immortality, or continued spiritual enlightenment. This is true happiness. Life is about becoming an ordinary human so that you can then become an extraordinary human. In application, this means a physically and spiritually healthy and long life. My Master *Li* lived to be over one hundred thirty years old and passed away in the year of two thousand and four. She was always in good shape, never even losing one single tooth. Her eyes could see in darkness and her ears could hear little things dropped on the ground from one hundred yards away. This is called super-nature, not supernatural. It is called healthy longevity. Many people should be able to live that long and stay that healthy.

Your concept of happiness is defined by whether you are striving for material or spiritual happiness. People say that great material accomplishments, and even more so great spiritual achievements, are happiness. However, true happiness is in living fully in the everyday, living fully in the every single moment. Looking for happiness will not bring it to you. Many people try too hard to find happiness, but what they look for is often on the material level. There are some people who look for spiritual happiness but they have no destiny or concept of what real happiness means.

Chapter 19

Choice Between Happiness and Pain

At the time I left China it was illegal to do so. An underground group arranged everything. I borrowed the thirty thousand dollars to get to the United States. Tao uses all forms, so I trusted that the Tao would bring me to the U.S. without risk. I crossed the Chinese continent by train and then, at the border I met with a large group of people. In the southwest of China we crossed into Burma at midnight on December 23, 1990. We jumped across the border with fifty-some people and ran quickly. Guards with machine guns could shoot at you from both sides of the border. Our Burmese rebel guides led us across with two machine guns, one at the front and one in the back. It such a dark night! Even though there was a trace of moonlight, it was very dark. Everyone else carried a small backpack but all I brought was a plastic bag with a few dried snacks. As we jumped across the border everyone ran for their own life. I was able to see we were on a very steep hill. I was able to run and see the path under me in a red color. I was able to see every rock, every hole and every bush. Although everyone else was falling all over the place, rushing and getting hurt, I was able to see. I held onto a few people from my village and said, "You follow me." After crossing, we traveled by foot for ten days, traveling the whole of Burma. We passed through very poor villages. Even so, this trip was fun and very spiritual for me. I learned from the experience. I had my purpose. My Master asked me to fulfill my mission to the West, to teach Taoism and healing arts.

Most of the fifty people were very rich. They just wanted to go to the West and were somewhat misled. They thought that in the United States there was so much money to be made. As we traveled through Burma, through the regular villages, we saw in the houses whole families in one bed, with one comforter. We would buy a skinny little pig to slaughter for food. There wasn't much food to be had, just a little steamed rice and a skinny pig for fifty people. Although the villagers were extremely poor they were happy. At times, I was so ashamed that I wanted to cover my face. I was ashamed for my group. But I knew that I had a purpose. I told our group, "Look at you, you want to go to the

West to look for your happiness in gold. Look at these people, this whole village. They have nothing. They suffer and are so poor, yet they are happy. Compared to them, you are ten thousand times richer and you still think you are so poor." I felt a certain degree of shame for myself as well, the needs of my family and the needs of my health, to come to the United States to take care of them. I felt bad for ever having felt like I was poor. When I saw those villages, I felt like I was really rich.

Because of my Kung Fu skills, I was able to help maintain integrity within the group, to keep people from fighting for food. No one could challenge me, so I was able to become the leader of our group of fifty. Had I not, people would have fought and killed each other over the food, over where to sleep, or over who was in the better place to lie down. I wasn't the official leader; I was just the person that people listened to and respected. One day we finally came to the Mekong River Delta. We hid along the Mekong River that crosses over three countries. We hiked through the triangle and then crossed into Bangkok, Thailand. A high government official was the smuggler in Thailand. He presented fake passports to all fifty of us. He overheard that I was a Taoist priest, a Kung Fu guy and a healer. This official was very rich and powerful, but still very loyal to his mother. His mother was sick. He asked if I could make a trip to heal his mother. In just two trips I healed his mother's disease. She was once again able to hear, speak, talk and smile. The official implored me to stay in Bangkok, to be his bodyguard. He offered his niece in marriage, his beautiful eighteen-year-old niece. If I stayed in Bangkok, he would pay me huge money to be his bodyguard, be a healer for his family and marry his niece.

I explained, "No, this is not my destiny. I need to go to the United States." I needed to go to teach, to build a temple there. So I resisted his offers and persuaded him to let me go; and to smuggle us through the airport with fake passports on a flight to Los Angeles. In a short period of time I went from starving and cold in the mountains of Burma, walking for ten days; and then, to a mansion in Bangkok. Most people would have said yes to this offer. He offered everything, money, power, a car and a wife. People from my countryside said I was stupid, a fool. But instead, I went to the United States. I arrived in Los Angeles and was immediately locked up in an immigration detention center. They locked me up because I had no passport. I had torn up the passport and flushed it down the toilet in the airplane. I was locked up for a total of eighteen days. The illegal smuggling group arranged for a lawyer to come in and get me out as a political asylum case.

While in detention, I made friends. It was the first time I saw people of different nationalities and heard other languages. I spoke no English. All I had was the one hundred dollars hidden under my belt. I believe in smiling though. I believe in heart-to-heart communication. I believe the smile and the heart communicate. I conversed by smiling and shaking hands with people, helping and healing. There were Black and Latin and Caribbean people, many were sick. I couldn't speak the verbal language but I was able to do healing. I became the unofficial healer in the detention center. It was fun to hear different languages, see the diverse culture and eat unusual foods. When I was given my first green salad, I thought, "What kind of food is this? It's not cooked. Are these people not educated? Why do

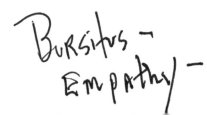

people eat raw food?" Now, of course, I eat salad too. I had no exact plan; I merely believed the Tao would guide me. I believed that I would meet people and that I would find my direction.

Happiness and pain are a choice of freedom of will. "*Dun Wu*" is a Chinese term used to describe a sudden breakthrough of mind and reality between the material world and the spiritual world. We have a free will to make the choice of happiness or pain. This is a self-choice without restriction. It is not a passive choice. It is an active choice, whether you realize it or not. When you raise the sword, your wisdom should kick in to make a wise choice, giving you to have the ability to drop the sword and become immortal in spirit. When you face all the obstacles of life you will learn to be a friend, to stand on the side of God and not the devil. This is a self-choice. Kindness is the original state of the human being. As long as you have this original conscience, you will always be able to make the wise choice to entertain life rather than to be entertained by life. Your spirit is like a cat and your life journey is like a rat. Does the cat play the rat or does the rat play the cat? It is a choice for everyone to make every day.

Although a person's mind may be unpleasant, life is not unpleasant. Life is what you make of it. If, in your mind, you choose for life to be unpleasant, then in your mind life will indeed be unpleasant. It is your choice to believe that life is unpleasant. That does not mean that the life associated with this choice is unpleasant, rather it is only the mindful choice that is unpleasant.

A second concept for you to develop is to go with the flow. *Tao* follows its nature. A cat, without a rat to play with, is a bored cat. A master, without a student, is not a master. A husband, without a wife, is not a husband. Don't kill the rat or you will no longer be a cat.

Never let the rat play the cat. Entertain your spirit to the best that you can. Refuse to be a half-assed person. It is not what you do; rather it is how you do it. When I first came to the United States, I was a Taoist priest, a master of Kung Fu, *Tai Chi*, *Qi Gong* and internal alchemy. I knew many things and I was very qualified about universal matters, but I needed a job to pay for the thirty thousand dollars that it cost me to come to the United States. The only job that I could get was at McDonald's, cooking hamburgers. I could choose to be miserable because this job was not what I trained all my life for. Instead, I chose to be happy. I used this time to perfect my skills of *Tai Chi* and to learn the English language. I practiced *Tai Chi* by placing ten hamburgers on the grill at once—laying the buns out quickly and gracefully with flow. It was fun! I thought it was fun because once I decided to take the job, I also knew that I might just as well make fun out of it. When you have integrity in doing a job, and you are responsible for the job, then you have fun. I was in charge of cooking, flipping McDonald's meat patties, cleaning the restaurant, cleaning the bathrooms, cleaning the stoves, throwing away old oil, the whole nine yards. In the early morning, around six o'clock, I would ride my bicycle in and start working. I received an hour break for eight hours of work, so it was very nice. I thought, "Why not enjoy myself." If I went back to the three months previous, I was a famous guy and now, here, three months later I was flipping burgers in this unhealthy food environment and at such low pay. I could have chosen to think of myself as a victim. But instead, I was happy! Four dollars and seventy-five cents per hour for eight hours a day was a lot of money compared to wages in China. So I enjoyed working every day. I smiled and learned. When it was very busy, I would ask my colleagues to step away and I would use my *Tai Chi* skills. I did not want them to get into my way. I picked up nine patties, put nine buns on the toaster and then put nine patties on the grill in one sweeping move. The grill was covered, one side with cooking patties and the other side with toasting buns. One strike of the tray on the grill and all the patties were on the grill. One more strike and the nine patties were all turned. I would flip nine patties onto the buns, then add whatever condiments they needed, wrap them and place them onto the trays. People thought, "That's a wild, funny Chinese Kung Fu dude doing hamburger flipping in the kitchen." I made my tasks into a workout training. Why not make good use of the time. I was having a good *Tai Chi* workout and I could make myself healthy all the while I was working. I became very good at my job so that they offered me an opportunity to be a manager. From this, I met people and started teaching. Within three years, I paid off my loan. You can let your work deplete your energy or you can allow your work to charge your energy! Life is supposed to charge your energy and not deplete it. When you curse your life or your job, then you curse yourself. Be passionate for life. Don't let darkness kill you. Always see the light at the end of the tunnel. Do your best without pressuring yourself. Think only of what is in front of you right at this moment.

Process: # 9: Write down the following four things:

Describe the happiest moment that you see coming into your life after today.

The most painful moment.

The most successful moment.

The most disappointing moment.

Crap just doesn't happen, rather you choose crap or you choose no crap. God possesses an abundance of wealth. You must ask yourself, "Am I the one to accept it or will I refuse it?" If you choose to refuse it, then don't choose to be a victim of God by saying "God, why do you refuse me?"

When you find yourself falling into a zone of your fear, get back into your comfort. What's most real is your own body. The illusion of fear is always created in your own fantasy mind. Take a deep breath to feel your most important gift, the gift that, "I am in my own body." Feel your fingers and feel your hands. Realize that you are not in a dream. Take a breath, jiggle your butt and tell yourself, "I am here!" These are the little things that you can control: "I am alive!" Feel and know that you are a living being. This is very important. Take the time to feel your heart beating and your breathing. This is your self-comfort zone. Once this is felt, then everything else becomes simple. You know that, this is real and you are real. Everything else is unreal. Knowing all of this, then you can be smart. Take care of what is real first! If you see it and smell it, then find your own way to get the apple. Getting the apple requires determination. The road will not provide for easy conditions, it is not a straight path. See and find your objective. What is it? Where is it? Simply brush away all the fake bubbles around you.

Following McDonald's, I worked three months for a defense contractor. I had to pay rent, repay my debt and send money back to my parents in China. After paying all this, I had about twenty dollars each week for food. So for one year I ate congee, a Chinese rice soup and dry peanuts. It was the only food at the market that I could recognize.

At the defense-contractor job, I was discriminated against because I was a foreigner. Although I was working hard and doing fast work, I was passed over for raises that instead went to a high school employee who was lazy and did poor work. When I inquired why, my supervisor fired me.

So, I thought, I have enough, I have my skill. I will not beg for a living; I will make a living. I will not beg for mercy; I am here to make mercy. And I thought, "I have my skills: *Tai Chi* skill, skill to do healing." I borrowed five hundred dollars to buy a massage table and I started working with one person. I was able to work with one client at a time, for forty-five dollars per hour doing energy healing.

I felt bad charging people money for energy healing because in my tradition, in my country, we do this spiritual work without charging. We give our heart; we give our skill to serve. But in Chinese tradition, people give back. People honor your heart and give you back what you need.

I thought forty-five dollars was a lot of money, but many people charge one hundred and fifty dollars just for a massage.

Though I felt bad that I had to charge money, I was self-employed and I had to make a living.

For a long time I explained to people, "I'm so sorry to go away from my tradition. I'm sorry I have to charge you this money. I have to pay for this table, the rent; I have to pay for electricity." I felt guilty for charging people money. But I vowed that I would keep charging the same amount for nine years.

Nine is my belief; it is the highest number of *Yang*. It is a power of dignity. I kept that promise. Many people came and my reputation spread widely. I healed much of disease, all kinds of disease. People from around the country came to me and I built up a reputation for healing.

You can't have a poor mentality to be a spiritual, happy person. Being alone is the ultimate joy. Don't feel guilt for wanting to be alone. Heaven includes the whole. God and the devil are never forced into your door. It is your choice to invite the devil. Love opens the door to God with true simplicity. Open the door to the devil with attachment. Do you want to be in league with God or with the devil? Using love or hate will automatically align you with either. If you never open the door to the devil, then the devil will not come in. There is no technique to chase the devil out. Reaffirm the Spirit, "Who am I?" You are multidimensional: the past, the present and the future, from great grandpa to great grandchild. You are the whole and you are the lineage.

This concept of change, self and selflessness is equal to *Tao*. Nothing less than one hundred percent you must believe that God is within. Then, whatever you wish will be granted.

When you say or think, "I am being tested," already you are acting like a victim. It is all in how you perceive things. Everything is fun; it is in your heaven. By stating that you are, "going," as opposed to, "growing" to heaven, you have already acknowledged that you are separated from heaven. It simply depends on what you believe, how you recognize the world; and this your life. To find hope and harmony with the purpose in your life, you must find consistency to guide you.

Let your conscience, the God within, guide you. Then there will be no place for the devil to know, or to recognize your world and your life. All of life, thoughts and actions have to be in line with your hope, your desire for the purpose of your life. Growing into heaven is the greatest, the ultimate spiritual fun. Beneath this, you are then supported by greater material fun.

Chapter 20

Choice is Based on the Quality of the *Yuan Shen*

From a humble beginning I built up. I now do seminars all over the world. For the first time, I have brought priests from the Wu Dang Mountain to the United States. I teach Taoism, healing and immortality training all over the United States and the world now. I am back to my intent. I left China and then found work at McDonald's. Now, once again, I am a healer and a lecturer. I lecture to crowds all over and I am in demand for speaking. This week alone I'll be in Florida, Las Vegas and Atlanta teaching *Tai Chi, Qi Gong*, healing, and Taoism. I have returned full circle, returning is the motion of the *Tao.* "Where you return is where your heart is." Always trust and listen to your heart. If you know what your passion is, then always follow that. I know my mission is my passion. I never take my eyes off my mission and so, I'm never disappointed when situations happen. You just do what feels right.

Many people struggle with making the right choice in their life. It is quite the challenge for those who wish to make that choice, but their spirit is just not capable. The quality and power of the *Yuan Shen* is based upon the quality and quantity of *Jing* and *Qi* through a lifetime. During your lifetime, stress, disease and emotions decrease the strength of the *Yuan Shen*, the original spirit. It just so happens that the *Yuan Shen* is the guide for your life's destiny. Although the subconscious mind knows what choice to make, the conscious mind often times takes control, and so the choice is often times made by intelligence at that moment. You will not make a wise choice based upon a weak spirit. It is extremely challenging for people addicted to bad habit and disease to be wise and make the right choice. You must exercise your will by combining physical, mental and spiritual cultivation step by step. In that way, you rebuild the power of *Yuan Shen*, eventually allowing you to make a great choice.

Appreciate your mother and father. You have a personal choice to make on how you perceive your parents. Be smart; don't judge them. Only then will you let your own children continue to enjoy their passion of life. If you treat your parents wrong, then your children will likewise treat you wrong. You are privileged and have been afforded great opportunity through the special gift of education. Family and community are like the soil for the tree, of which the root came from the parents. Be accepting, not intolerant. Life is a living heaven, not a living hell.

Happiness is the only purpose of life! How do you face disease and death? Before you go to battle, if you turn your head to look back, then you are already dead. Do not look back or behind! You have only the now to work with, so work with this moment rather than the tomorrow or the yesterday. You can't construct a house before you have the blueprint. All you have is the now, the present. Money is the transformation of virtue that you sow. Be careful not to label. What you wish for becomes reality. Deliver hope, not death. Everybody deserves the opportunity to live and to die by their own accord. At any given moment you can receive enlightenment.

You must trim excessive emotional fat. Never just cover your butt, because no matter how hard you contrive, your master will see through the cover. By being natural, you show God that you are the one who can ride the dragon. Choose wisely, what you want. Do not try to cover your weaknesses and definitely, do not defend them. The best approach is to expose your weaknesses. Exposing weakness only takes two seconds; whereas, covering your weaknesses takes a lifetime to defend.

Humans are different from saints and saints are different from immortals. As long as you are human, your measure for being spiritual will be based upon the three Taoist treasures of conscience, mercy and forgiveness. The quality of each determines what level of human being you are. If your spirituality remains in the intellectual realm, then it is not true spirituality. Don't have a rigid understanding. Access your heart to feel conscience, mercy and forgiveness. You must be human first before you can achieve true spirituality. Human spiritual is the same as immortal spiritual, only the quality is different. Don't fantasize about who you are. Don't fantasize about how spiritual you are. Just be human.

There is a story about *Ji Gong*, a monk who is a Buddha. He had come down to earth to enlighten Buddhist practices. Chinese Buddhism had become very rigid. As the story is told, *Ji Gong* wanted to tease the people and teach them that it's about the heart and spirit connection, not about appearance. So he came to earth looking like a bum. He arrived at the gate of the temple asking for a place to sleep. The priest told him, "No, you are too dirty" and they locked him out. Despite being locked out, *Ji Gong* was found inside the temple. Again and again he came into the temple despite having been locked out. The priest and others could not keep him out. Finally, they decided to let him stay, but only on the condition that *Ji Gong* would stay hidden. They did not want him to be involved in temple gatherings because, as they told *Ji Gong*, "You are a disgrace!" They also gave *Ji Gong* the impossible task of raising enough money to reconstruct a new temple. He was given only thirty days to complete this task. Although the deadline was short, until up to the last hour *Ji Gong* did nothing but drink and sleep. The priests clamored to kick him out, so *Ji Gong* brought them all to the well and performed a chant. "Wood Log" flowed from the well in great abundance.

Don't be rigid in your thoughts of who and what spirituality should look like. Don't judge what you see. Preconceived notions of what spirituality looks like are often deceiving. Don't decide what a monk is "supposed" to be.

"Wine and meat goes through my intestines, but the Buhda stays in my heart."

Do you truly have God in your heart? Do you truly have *Tao* in your heart? Tao is in you. It's not a question of using intelligence. You can't look for God based on the limitations of your intellect. God is not found in your judgments. You will never find it there. Every human has the same common sense; that being the heart, but instead people vigorously defend what they believe based upon their own intelligence. This makes for an illusory pattern.

You become a "smiling tiger" when you are forced into someone else's paradigm. Sometimes, when people are virtuous and wise in spiritual power, they may use this to get what they want. This is a sugarcoated bullet. It manipulates people and attacks their spirit. While some people may attack with force, others attack with intent and still others attack with power. This happens every single day. Will you be a victim of it? You have the choice to say no, or to accept it. If you're weak in spirit, people will use pity to take advantage of your mercy. If they see that you are forgiving, they may take advantage of this. You are a fool to forgive on the third time. It's okay to forgive once or twice, but on the third time, accept no more. Others may use love to manipulate. It happens every day. This is killing you softly. Stay awake and stay wise! Make your choices. Say, "No" and be brave. Only you know yourself. You know your comfort zone, so honor it.

Take the time to know your comfort zone. Is it big or small? Is it solid or is there flexibility depending on the circumstance? Is it loose or tight? Maintain a spiritual comfort zone and be firm with it. Stay with what you believe is right. Your comfort zone can be reasonably flexible, but it needs to be firm at the same time. If you can't honor your own comfort zone, then others certainly will not honor it. If you can't honor your own comfort zone, then you are not honoring yourself. It can be very hard to say, "No," but you must practice it. Practice with a partner and see if you can make them say yes to you. The sugarcoated bullet always comes when you least expect it. It comes when you lose your guard. So be conscious!

Process # 10: Close your eyes and envision your dream house. Next see yourself in the city; taking a vacation; go to the mountains. Really see these dialectically, logically and illogically. After each, open your eyes and write down what you see.

Why should you practice this exercise? The dream house represents your goal. Family is a good string attached to you. Friends show too much attachment to temptation. The stillness of doing this gives birth into the action. Where are you coming from? The concept of home is your shelter. The concept of self is your spirit. City represents your work life. Vacations tell you how you entertain your spirit. Going to the mountain is a spiritual journey, so pay attention to what you see and hear. How do you feel?   The return is your reunion. If you still have the preference to choose, then your spirit is not strong. Your spirit walks ahead of time, so you already know what you want. Get clear, a dragon can't fly without a head.

Chapter 21

Emotion and Desire are the Blockage of Happiness

Your fears are illusions. When you run from them you keep them alive. Attack fears before they get you. This concept needs to be understood by your spirit. Taoism teaches you how to discover your hidden dragon. Can you ride the hidden dragon? Make sure that you stay on the dragon. Hold on tight and enjoy the ride! If you can do this, then you can become the dragon. Discover the dragon. Cultivate body, mind and spirit to ride the dragon. You must be able to discover and face emotions. Know who you really are, then you can go deep. When you understand the relationship between spirit body and physical body you can understand the purpose of living and walking through this life journey. There is no more saying, "life is a living hell." You project your thoughts into the universe in every moment and it makes a mark on the universe. You fight for recognition and approval. We all constantly do this. Perhaps you do it unconsciously, but you do it. Become more conscious now. Be careful what you are projecting. Every thought is energy. Your emotion is energy. Understand this and then reverse it to see the internal impact.

Process # 11: Write down three procedures to solve emotions and fears, and to gain hopes.

Process # 12: Express your feeling for three minutes, but no longer. This is what it is to be human. To resist or restrain emotions is not being human. Just do not hold onto the emotions after the three minutes.

Process # 13: Write three things that you absolutely don't want to lose. Write this on top of the list of fears and hopes.

In your life, the rat is equal to attachments to life, desires, emotions and cravings. Once you are lured into these attachments you are entertained by the rat. Once entertained, the rat continues to suck you in. Your cat, the spirit, has the ability to either kill the rat, or to perhaps keep the rat around as entertainment. The cat can eat the rat, but you are a fool to kill your audience. If the cat eats all of the rats, then there are no more rats to entertain your spirit. Only fools think that the world is perfect. It is both perfect and imperfect. Does the rat play the cat or does the cat play the rat? Every penny spent attaching to desire and material attachment makes your self a slave of the material and therefore, a slave of the rat. The rat becomes the master; the emotion becomes the master. Do emotions play you, or do you play the emotions? Perhaps they both play each other and come into harmony. The cat and the rat can play and enjoy the game, not unlike in the children's cartoon "Tom and Jerry."

As soon as you "have" a possession, you have something to lose. This comes from logic. Logic is fifty percent true. So live in another way, live in the fifty percent illogic. Your spirit needs to be exercised. You need to live and let live. The more you attach to something, the more you think that you should possess it. This leads to vulnerability and increases the pressure to live more freely.

Process # 14: Open your palm and grasp the air.

Can you grasp the air? No! When hands are open you have the air, but when you try to grab and possess the air you lose it. When you try to possess a concept, when you try to possess an object, you lose it. It is okay to enjoy the air. It is okay to breathe it in and to breathe it out, but if you only breathe air in, without breathing it out, you will die and then consequently you still lose the air. That which you let go of, you get.

Follow your nature without logic. When you observe, observe! When you participate, participate fully. When you allow yourself to be vulnerable, you allow yourself to be played by the rat. Desire and attachment overcome your spirit, making you a slave of possession and as a result you lose your freedom. Likewise, when you possess your freedom, you lose freedom. Notice how the desire plays you.

How many rats do you have that will play your cat in your life? Look back to your list of fears and hopes. Are these fears and hopes a rat? The more you focus on what you want, the more you lose it. You can have both. However, if you must have, then life becomes much more difficult. By craving, you lose the ability to enjoy and weakness comes. Your wants weaken your spiritual power. Ability and joy is taken away.

Attach, detach and then attach again. Attachments are not bad, just be able to let go and don't get entangled in your attachment. Play around with them. See and not see; do and not do. Be on the third side of the coin. You need to acknowledge the self and the selflessness. Then, you can find another self. Beyond this new understanding of self is another self. This fourth understanding is the hidden dragon.

You create your own environment of fear. Preserve the integrity of spirit and be in the moment rather than in the fear of the future. When a real fear does emerge in the present, deal with it. Just don't live in a constant fear of the future. The future does not exist, only now does. Live in the high quality of the integrity of life without the fear of something to lose. You can't change the world; however, you can work on yourself to change.

Subconscious behavior is the most difficult and challenging behavior to delete. Most people don't think that they are good enough. They vigorously defend fear. Instead, I ask that you nurture the fragile immature spirit to refine it. You can refine spirit to receive wealth. Feel the integrity and quality to spend the money. You have so much to be appreciative for. God has given you the gifts of sight, hearing and bodily functions. Be appreciative of the gift. It is an absolute precious gift from God. In the cave there is no reason to complain even though there is no water or no hot shower. You ignore the gifts that God has given while continuing to ask for extra gifts from the devil—the sugarcoated bullet from the devil. Playing with the devil, you become a slave. Don't check in your conscience. Never negotiate with God. Choose to make the wise choice. The wrong choice is always slavery. Don't get stuck on top of the fence by not being clear about your choice. Make a crystal clear choice. A human's original nature is conscience. God conscience is equal to universal wisdom.

When you are very emotional and feel like a victim, you don't have self-worth or self-value. You base your thoughts on the concept that you "deserve" and as a result you ask for discounted integrity, blindfolded integrity. This is why others still don't respect you. You are not in your heart and not in line with God. Pure heart and soul gain integrity and respect. A victim doesn't ask for it. If you ask for it the devil will bow. However, if you pretend that you are God, then you are in line with the devil. Many people demand respect by saying, "I have value. I am worth it!" This is the wrong time and way to do it. The devil attaches even more. Demanding a title or respect is like playing with the devil. The devil never wants to play with God. The more you demand, the more respect you lose. Don't tell me I am not good enough. If you want to have your children eat an apple, then you too must eat with enthusiasm.

Are you the entertainer of your life or is life entertaining you? What do you choose? Life doesn't go by what you want. Entertain and look beyond. Look and live in both dimensions and then live in the third dimension. Live beyond the spiritual and material realms. Live in the place of the hidden dragon. You understand this after you have begged on your feet for three months.

I am officially of the 14th generation disciple of the Wu Dang *Zhang San Feng* branch. *Zhang San Feng* was the creator of Wu Dang *Tai Chi*. Along with my Taoist brother, we are the highest-ranking priests on the mountain: we are of the 14th generation. I'm also 25th generation *Long Men* (Dragon Gate) branch under my Master *Li*. I am her successor, disciple, unofficially but officially, because I was never registered in the Wu Dang Mountain. Now, years later, after I returned and showed who I am, what I know, they honored me and gave me the title of 14th generation and 25th generation Taoist priest. The Taoist Association knows who I am and that my mission is in line with the Taoist Association's in the Mountain. They gave me the title of Wu Dang Official Exclusive Representative in America and the exclusive representative for Wu Dang Local Government.

The largest building on Wu Dang Mountain was constructed during the *Ming* Dynasty. It was the Imperial Temple. Officially, they only started construction in 1612. But even 1000 years before that, there were many Taoist priests who came to Wu Dang Mountain as hermits to live in the caves or to live in little temples scattered around the mountain, cultivating immortality. After construction began in 1612, over one hundred building groups were constructed. Over 300,000 people came to the Mountain and were employed by the Imperial government to build the temples.

Wu Dang is a mystical mountain, one of the sacred mountains of China and the birthplace of Taoism. Even *Lao Tsu* went to Wu Dang for cultivation. *Lao Tsu* is the author of the "*Tao Te Ching*," one of the most translated books in the world, along with the Bible.

My mission has never changed: to build a Taoist monastery, to introduce the ancient Taoist way of life and philosophy to this modern world, to help people, to introduce them to a way to live with nature, a way to honor themselves and to find peace within themselves. In addition to building the Temple, my mission is to teach the ancient metaphysical arts to the world. I believe the ancient secrets should be shared with the world equally: peaceful living, healthy longevity and a healthy mind.

Tao is an interesting concept. The more you think you get it, the more you lose it. You cannot describe it; you can only feel it. However, when you think that you can feel it, that's when you lose it. See the dialectic? You're right and I'm right too. It's just the way you look at it

Take things lightly and let it go. Let the heart relax. When the heart is active, then you are feeling, "My feelings are hurt." When you take away the paper, there is no use for ink.

Stop giving people paper to hurt your feelings with. Ninety-nine point nine percent of the time you crave for the material: attention, success, beauty and acceptance. We always crave for something. These are the seven emotions and six desires. The price is so heavy to pay for your cravings.

There is a "Big Dipper Story," the story of Wu Dang Taoism and Zhen Wu the Truth Warrior God. One day the Jade Emperor was in heaven when, suddenly he saw, far away below the clouds, five colored beams of light shooting up from earth to heaven. He was very surprised and asked his prime minister "What is this? Can you go take a look?" The prime minister went to the edge of the clouds and looked down to the earth. He came back and reported, "The five streams of light come from a golden tree on Wu Dang Mountain in middle earth China. They are the spirits of the five elements. When they beam up, the power of harmony is shooting straight through the universe all the way to heaven."

"Wow," the Jade Emperor thought, "I have all the treasure of the universe, but I've never seen this light. I should go look at that." At that moment, ego and desire stirred in his chest. Immediately, one of his ninety-nine souls separated from him and went into a queen's belly to become a baby. The queen's baby was prince of the pure happiness kingdom. He was very powerful and very smart. He knew all the books, wrote poems and was interested in alchemy. At fourteen years old, the prince didn't want to become the next ruler of the kingdom. So he rode off to Wu Dang Mountain to cultivate alchemy and immortality. His parents were close by and caught him by the sleeve, pleading,

"Please come back! We can't do without you!" But he answered, "No" and cut his sleeve. The sleeve dropped to the ground and became the river known as Broken Sleeve River.

He had heard that Wu Dang was mystical and knew that a golden tree grew there. When the prince saw the beautiful and powerful tree and saw the light beaming from it, he dismounted his horse and started to kneel down to pray to the tree. But the prince's soul was that of no other than the Jade Emperor. So when the Five Elements in the Tree saw that the Jade Emperor had come to kneel down they were scared and ran off to the edges of the universe, as they could not have him kneel to them. They disappeared to the five corners of the universe.

The prince went to a temple called Prince Slope Temple to cultivate for twenty and then thirty years. He was so deep. The first twenty years were so challenging that he became discouraged wanted to walk away. Additionally, he was so very lonely. He was by himself, which was so different from the prince's life he had been use to. He wanted to go back to his life as a prince, but a Goddess saw the prince discouraged and became worried. The universe wanted the soul back. So the goddess disguised herself as an elderly lady, sitting by the well, holding a big steel rod and grinding it into a needle. The prince saw this and asked, "Old lady, why are you here grinding this big metal pole?" She replied, "Oh, young man I'm just sitting here all day to make a needle." "How long will this take?" He asked and she replied, "As long as you make up your mind, one day the needle will form." The prince heard this and suddenly he became enlightened. "Thank you so much! I will continue to cultivate Tao," he said to her.

The prince spent forty-two years in Wu Dang Mountains cultivating and meditating. He was so dedicated to the art that he didn't realize he had already accomplished the Tao and had become immortal. Forty-two years on earth was equivalent to four and two tenths days in heaven. And as long as the soul of the Jade Emperor was not complete, his heavenly work was not being done. The heavenly immortals and gods wanted his soul back so that the Jade Emperor could be complete to administer heaven and keep it in order. So they conspired with Kuan Yin Lao Mu and came up with a plan on how to bring him back.

Kuan Yin Lao Mu entered the prince's dream one night and said to him, "There is a bell by the cliff. If you can throw a coin through the large hoop that hangs in front of it, and hit the bell three times, it means that you have a common affinity with Tao and you can accomplish immortality." When he woke from his dream he figured that with all of his training he should easily be able to complete the task.

The following day he came to the cliff. He picked up three coins and threw one, two, three, but all three times failed to hit the bell. He thought, "Well, my common affinity with the Tao must be gone. I must have no common affinity." After forty-two years of cultivating he was so disappointed and decided to leave the mountain. He came to a platform to comb his hair. Suddenly, Kuan Yin Lao Mu, disguised as a beautiful young lady, showed up and said, "Can I comb your hair? I'm lost in the mountains and I'm afraid. Tigers and wild animals chase me. I want to stay with you. I can marry you. You can protect me."

The prince replied, "I have spent forty-two years in the

mountain cultivating Tao and I have never had a woman around, nor have I ever been touched by a woman. So although I don't have a common affinity with the Tao, I still do not want anything to do with women." The lady started crying and said, "I'm alone and I'm insecure here. You don't want me and I have nowhere to go." She ran to a high cliff and jumped, plunging down to the earth. The Prince said, "I have no common affinity with the Tao. She died for me, and I have nothing to give but my life." So, he ran to the cliff and launched himself off. As soon as he plunged down, five dragons of different colors appeared and held him in the clouds. He turned his head to look and there was Kuan Yin Lao Mu standing in the cloud. Finally he understood that he had already become immortal. The heavenly carriage came, the heavenly music played and the dragons and phoenix flew around, and took him up to heaven.

His one soul reunited with the Jade Emperor so that the Jade Emperor was complete again. The Jade Emperor said the Prince was such a good warrior that he gave him the title, Zhen Wu, Truth Warrior. He put Zhen Wu in charge of 300,000 heavenly troops to sweep negativity and evil out of the universe on every Wednesday and Sunday. Wu Dang is the birthplace of the immortal. To gain immortal energy consider cultivating in Wu Dang where there is magic.

Cultivation encompasses a process of forgiveness. You don't need the baggage of your emotions and desires. You no longer need to carry them for the rest of the journey. It's a process of refreshment. Let go of the baggage. Stop feeling like, "I need to feel the emotions so that I know I am alive. It makes up my identity. Without the emotions, I am nobody. I need an explanation for my unhappy life." Just say no. This type of thinking and action is merely another way to play the victim. If you hold onto the baggage, then you really don't want to heal. You can't feel the joy of life. You don't know what it's about. Holding onto pain, is a very dangerous thought process for you, so don't do it! We hold emotions as an excuse. It's like an insurance policy that, at any guilty moment, you can pull out so as to not take responsibility.

Do you often have a particular excuse that you use? When you have a lack of self-confidence, you will always try to find the reason for it. Excuses come from a lack of self-confidence. Another symptom for lack of self-confidence is fantasy. We may go to the extreme opposite end. In the movie: "Runaway Bride," she kept falling from one relationship into another, always finding an excuse. Females tend to put down other females; whereas, males tend to use intellectual strength against each other, thinking, "I'm better than." Look to see what you often do, how you often perform. When you use excuses, you lose track of your life journey goal. The cost to fight for your lack of self-confidence is steep. You give up on your real goal of why you live.

Be extraordinary by rising above your emotions and realizing that being ordinary is a gift from God. With this understanding, you become extraordinary. Remember the path and the purpose of your journey. The more you practice, the more clear the path becomes. You are here to learn how to detach from the ordinary intelligence and to attach to the wisdom intelligence. When you talk about and identify your deeply held emotions, it helps to have *"Dun Wu,"* a sudden breakthrough. Talk about them not so much as to hold onto them, but instead, to bring them out into the light so that you no longer fear them and can let go of them.

Chapter 22

Disciplined Effort Leading to a Good Choice

When I was ten years old, before my three month walk out of the temple to be a beggar learning about life, my master brought me outside the temple to look at "The Golden Tree." The Golden Tree was right in front of our temple. That is why our temple was called Golden Flower Temple. She said, "Chen, little boy, jumping monkey." She always called me jumping monkey because I was young and my attention, my mental intention, was all over the place. She said, "Jumping monkey, look at that Golden Flower Tree and tell me, what do you see?"

I immediately said, "I see a tall, magnificent tree," and so, she asked again, "What do you see?" Three times she asked and each time I described what I saw on this tree and how I felt about this tree and each time I got a bamboo knock on the head. She intimated, "Too much mind. You are a jumping monkey with too much mind, you are a monkey." So I asked, "Master, I saw a tree. How can I not see a tree?" She knocked me on my head again. Every time she asked the question, I saw something and described it and she kept knocking me on the head—many, many times on the head.

By the end, everything in front of my eyes disappeared, I was busy trying to find something, I had been hit so many times, I was dizzy and I was trying so hard, and then, suddenly there really was nothing in front of me. So, for the last answer I said, "Master, now I see nothing, I really see nothing!" and she said, "Okay, Monkey, now your monkey mind is settled. Your monkey has finally settled down." So I asked, "Um, Master could you tell me what I really learned from this lesson? Why all of a sudden did my mind become blank? Why did I see nothing and think nothing? Why was my head completely empty?" And she replied, "You see a tree, you don't see. See and not see without attachment to any need."

So, I had a measure of enlightenment and a breakthrough and understood the journey that I am in, the technique that I was learning and the alchemy that I was learning. I understood that all you see can be real, but all it does is blindfold your conscious, blindfold your pre-heaven spirit. All the intelligence that you gather from the outside only entertains your post-heaven spirit. The more you fill up your head, the more confused you are, the more stress you cause. Then, you have no room to go into the emptiness, to feel the stillness. The foundation for the peacefulness and stillness going toward alchemy training fails.

You will not succeed at alchemy if you don't find the ground of stillness. In Chinese, we say, *"Dui Jing Wu Xin."* *"Dui"* is facing, *"Jing"* is scenery or life obstacle, *"Wu"* is nothing and *"Xin"* is mind and intention. Face all the scenery or life scenarios without any intention, without any mind attached to it. When you meditate and you see things internally; illusion, feeling, voices that might be heard, or odors that may get to your nose, those intuitions can raise your ego and desire and your conscious mind constantly tries to study and analyze. All this causes stress in your life. The more you can get out of the need for entertaining those scenarios, the better stillness you will obtain. If, when facing all life's obstacles, we are able to go beyond and not attach to the obstacles, taking them lightly and not attaching to all the byproducts from this stress, then life will be better, more tranquil and peaceful. A better joy will come to you.

The boat rises with the tide. Learn to follow what is your nature. Identify the blockage of life. Understand, accept and detach from emotional and physical blockage. Increase the quantity and quality of *Jing Qi*. Nourish the *Yuan Shen*. It is a disciplined effort. Progress starts slowly but the result is permanent. Once you experience the joy and happiness from everyday cultivation you make better and better choices in your own life's journey. At last, you have increased wisdom to enjoy a happy life.

You are the window of your own happiness. True candles burn to the last drop of wax. Love living! The Chinese character for *Tao* means, the head walks. First walk the talk. Set an example first. Life is happiness! Open the window for children. The more you think you can't do something, then the more likely that you will not do it. You are picky about what you buy for yourself, so why would you settle for a half-baked product from yourself. Do one thing well first! If you can do one thing well, then you can do two, three and four things well. It is the subconscious mind that prevents you from flying to heaven. People become so attached to their past that they treat their past as their child. The past becomes their safe haven preventing them from moving into the now. Have compassion!

Avoid the "if" philosophy. How often do you use, if? Any use of if is too often. Can you please give me one instance when if gave you something? If I had more, if that didn't happen, if I knew about it. "If" means never. "If" is just a pathetic excuse. If sets up the tone for failure, the tone for unhappiness. You keep doing this even though it sounds so pathetic because you don't listen to yourself. Develop the skill of listening to yourself when you talk. Then, you will understand the feeling of putting yourself in other people's shoes. "If" means you have no trust at all in yourself—no trust and no self worth. You automatically disassociate with your God spirit. You put yourself in line with the devil. Please replace "if" with "when." See how this brings the fire back to you! It's very dangerous to say "if."

Process # 15: Listen to yourself and find out what "if" sentence you use the most.

Again, can you pretend that everyone knows your subconscious mind? Do you really think people can't read your thoughts? When you pretend that everyone knows, then you will be very compassionate and loving. By pretending, now you know that your subconscious mind has poison. As you practice more, intent and thought become the same. Practice more! This process delivers unbelievable power. This is a *Tai Chi* thought. Then, when you do "push hands" you can catch people's intent before thought arises.

Practice and live daily with the three "D's:" devotion, dedication and discipline. Once you know that this is your path, that this is the purpose of your life, you must follow these three D's. After you practice for some time, you realize this is your true nature. Setting your goal is the jewel of *Tao*. Once you find it, be dedicated, devoted and disciplined toward it. To know internal alchemy, you have to meditate every day. You have to create the frequency to make it happen, or you will undermine the result. This is the discipline. It's very easy to find an excuse. Many times this excuse is a fantasy. Practicing must be in your blood and your soul. If you practice *Tao* as a fashion—just to fit in—it will not serve your purpose. Genuine discipline is required. Wear the fashion, but it must have a meaning to you. It's not a fashion. Knowing where you are from, why you are here and knowing that, "I am my master," then you know that there is a step-by-step approach to get there. Taoist philosophy is practical. This means that you need to practice.

This country is all about giving freedom to children. You have to herd a child and guide them, but not hurt them. Children need an adult to guide them. Parents live and teach through example. Live in your own conscience. You, as parents, are the window to the world of the children's joy and happiness. Show and live it. Living as a parent, every day you are obligated to show your children the joy of living and also, show them the reality of living. Don't paint the wrong picture for children. Don't agree with giving too much democracy. Otherwise, they have the wrong idea of the world. Disciplined effort is needed!

Chapter 23

Follow Your Heart and Make Your Choice

The heart is the master of all the organs. It is the foundation of your original spirit. We all carry the treasure of *Tao* in our heart. Unlock the treasure box and allow your heart to Shine. You are capable and able to make your own choice. Your heart and your spirit will guide you to the right path, or door, to your ultimate freedom in your home.

Process # 16: Ask yourself, "How much have I compromised in my life?"

If you agree with the principle of *Tao*, then you have to walk the talk. There is no manual to point out the way, only principles to teach. Do not try to broadcast what you have been taught. Be satisfied knowing that this is for you. There is no need to broadcast. Broadcasting suggests that you are merely seeking affirmations that you are on the correct path. If you seek to be told that you are on the right path, then God will choose someone to affirm you regardless of whether you truly are or not, so don't seek to be affirmed.

We all know how to make choices. It is called internal knowing. Can you be consistent in your choice making? Can you assert your willpower? We make choices by asserting our willpower. Either you are devoted to your choice, or you are not. You can always turn from your choice, but be devoted to the choice until that moment you choose to make a turn from your choice. Your choice should always match your goal; it should always match your dream. Make all your choices so that they match your goals and dreams.

Many years ago, one of the last Taoist priests to become immortal was on Wu Dang Mountain. He had cultivated for over thirty years and was very good with *I-Ching*. He became immortal and knew it was time to depart for heaven. On the day of his departure he put on a nice uniform, lit candles on his altar and meditated; all the while, he looked and waited for the immortals to come and eat with him. He waited until morning.

Waiting, waiting, waiting! In the middle of the day, a poor farmer came by and said, "You have a lot of food and I am very hungry. May I eat food with you?" The priest replied, "No, it is a big day for me. The immortals will come to eat with me." The farmer readily agreed, "Oh yes, it is indeed your big day. I will wait and perhaps afterwards I could share whatever food remains when you have finished." The priest consented.

And so, they waited and waited, and nothing happened, no one came. "Something is not right," the priest said. "I calculated for him to arrive at twelve noon and he never came. Please share my food with me," the priest said. The farmer agreed. The priest surmised, "I need to go to another place," and so, he returned to the temple to recalculate the arrival of the immortal. It was only then that he realized that the farmer was his immortal. He thought to himself, "Surely he will come again tomorrow." So once again, he went through the same process. This time around, another *Taoist* priest showed up. The waiting priest shared with him his attitude about becoming immortal. The second Taoist priest told him, "You are waiting for nothing. You need to chop your ego and only then will you become immortal." The second priest knew that as long as there is ego, there is no chance to become immortal.

Are you expecting a certain form to show up in life? It is not in your head, or your ego that you will find a breakthrough to God or *Tao*. I'll leave you some space to think about this. Some people have great passion; they hunger with passion to do something for the world. But you must ask yourself, "Are you capable? Are you ready? Are you the one to save the world?" Think of Hercules' holding the world while both legs are shaking.

Is he a hero? Raise your hands up and hold the sky. Notice how your legs shake.

How many of you use your ego and take on more responsibility than your ability allows you to be capable of handling? It is not shameful to take a deep breath, to take a pause. There are many victims for you to save but only one hero to live. Do you get it? People take responsibilities so seriously: this is why we are so messed up! You need to take rest. Get out of your head and into your heart!

Take these opportunities in logic and illogic. Life does not come as you expect it. So you have to keep the door of your heart always open. You can shut your eyes, as eyes can fool you. Keep your heart open and connected to your gut. Then, your logical mind won't interfere with what your gut tells you. Otherwise your three opportunities can pass so easily because you are stuck in your own logical world and you allow no opportunity for the illogical. *Tao* only gives you three opportunities. Grasp the opportunity with all your heart! These are the black dragon, the white dragon and the ingredients to make the third dragon. One creates two, two creates three and three creates ten thousand. You take two steps back and on the third step you lose your chance.

Many religions dominate with a fancy name or a fancy banner. People invariably buy into it. There is a certain strange behavior that is associated with spirituality. For example: they might say, "Don't eat meat." What if I put one thousand chickens in your home? You are so busy to point the finger at a concept that you will starve. You look out at the world through a keyhole and see only a piece of the sky. You insist on allowing yourself to have limitations. Understand that you limit your view from the keyhole. Don't be stubborn by advancing your pathetic behavior throughout your life. We are too willing to lose our identity for something that is an illusion. What is your true mission? You may be subconsciously disconnecting your heart from the mission. You may disassociate. You may reason, "I need to make a mission trip to save lives." Meanwhile, you forget that your backyard is on fire. You try so hard to be a hero. Ask yourself what happens when you come home? You lose your home, your life and your identity. Is being in your head and being a hero worth losing your home? This is what I mean about Hercules. He holds the world all the while his legs are shaking and he pees his pants. Learn to be a little selfish. It's okay to be selfish because you understand your children want to grow old with you.

I never put my students and my friends in a position that I have never been in. I have done this. I have tried to hold the sky up. I felt such a giggle; it was such a joy. I just wanted to share it with others. Joy is a contagious disease that can cure even the devil. Everyone has three opportunities for a life change. After that you fall back to reincarnation. The opportunity can be an event, a person, a movie or a book. These opportunities can come in direct or indirect experiences of life. It's important that you be aware so that you can seize the opportunity. Listen eagerly and follow. You can very easily overlook and Chinese-English can make you lose the translation. But when you listen, if you slow down your thoughts, you will hear. Sometimes you need to listen to a Master; sometimes from nature; sometimes from space and sometimes from an ordinary beggar on the street.

Wisdom comes from all kinds and forms, different timing, different form and different event. When you resort only to logical thinking, the wisdom can only come from the person in a strange robe.

Here is a paradox for all seekers, "A monk who sits in front of a Buddha statue chanting and hitting a wood fish to calm his mind, has a mouth, but does not have a heart." Chanting and praying done without awareness, is not genuine.

PART V

How do I Enjoy Life?

Chapter 24

Return to Simplicity

Shakespeare tells us that life is a play and that we are all actors or actresses in this magical play. Most people are so attached to the character they portray that they are unwilling to take off the mask to face reality. Living in fantasy and illusion can only suffocate the true self. Learn to face life with conscience, mercy and forgiveness. Then, there is no dust that needs to be cleaned and there is no stress to experience. Seek immortality rather than seeking or dwelling in the stress of humanity. From complication return to simplicity, nurturing stillness brings us to the state of unity between self and the universe. This is how you enjoy your material life and the spiritual life. *Taoism* is a practical philosophy that brings you a simple, practical understanding of humanity, pointing out a path to immortality.

There are eighteen methods in this chapter, eighteen tools for cultivating virtue and cultivating essential nature to take you home. This is the way you entertain life, this is the way you enjoy life. We use practical *Taoist* philosophy and theory to prescribe a way to open our body, mind and spirit to enjoy life. This is the way to increase your capacity and ability to feel joy. Cultivate essential nature to break through. Breaking through the mind is one of the most important steps of returning home. Even the best vehicle needs a wise person to drive it. The pilot of a supersonic jet has to have super skills to fly into heaven. This chapter provides a manual for the supreme joy, giving you the most wisdom to entertain life. It is a manual that gives the technique of joy. Looking inside to your "master within" is the way for you to entertain life.

Process: # 16: Take a pause in your life! Pause to find out where you are emotionally. As you did earlier in this book, list three emotions that hurt you most, for example: anger, trust, grief, fear, love. Then list the three hopes that you would like to accomplish most in life. If you truly want to change, you must identify and share where you are currently stalled. Finally, identify three procedures you can use to deal with emotions and hopes. You must pause and identify where things are broken, then take the time to lick the wounds. Pause, identify and lick wounds!!!

Chapter 25

The Power of Forgiveness

Forgiveness is one of the three treasures of *Tao*. Learn to forgive yourself first in order to detach from the feeling of being a victim. Make the choice to enjoy life rather than to hold onto and suffer from emotions. In doing this, you can bring back your original nature. When you no longer hold hatred or other emotion in your heart, your spirit shines in simplicity. Joy fills your heart, and then you are able to forgive anybody at any time and anywhere, unconditionally. This forgiveness will help bring you back to the right path, allowing you to cultivate stillness in your life, enabling you to have a better opportunity in seeking immortality.

Process # 17: Write a one-page letter to the person with whom you have the most blockages.

You are human so you are allowed to have three minutes of pain. Then, in the fourth minute, do a table dance to rid yourself of the pain. Don't punish yourself for having emotions, but also, do not become addicted to the emotions. Allow for the opportunity to express what is in your heart and soul. Then, having done so, release the emotions. Just because you learn these techniques does not mean that you stop being human and stop having emotions that arise. For the first three minutes, you are human. Then for the next three minutes, you are spirit once again, entertaining life. Allow for the transformation from the ordinary to the extraordinary. The wise person is always able to see that imperfection is what allows them to be perfect. Without appreciating the devil, you never have the opportunity to know God. The devil will always come back. Without the devil, there is no rat to play for the cat. Don't expect the devil to fully leave you. That does not mean that it has to take away your passion for life.

Process # 18: Are you able to forgive those who are absolutely unforgivable? How? Search into your life. What is the most unforgivable event in your life? Identify that most unforgivable event and ask your gut, "Can you forgive?" Then, ask yourself, "How to forgive?" The challenge is to make peace with this event within seventy-two hours from now. This is not just an illusion to imagine, you must really do it. You must pick up the phone and have that conversation.

There is a deep scar in your heart. Can you forgive those who, in your mind, are absolutely unforgivable? God looks for what is true in the heart, the true heart. Deep scars such as rape and violence take away the joy and happiness. You are not able to trust and may carry anger towards people and life. Then, you start to not pay attention to life. You must learn to forgive the unforgivable. Do not allow the tragic moment to take away your self-respect and what you are capable of. Tragic moments are meaningless, so you don't need to search why it happened. Don't use the "why" technique. Just work with it and wipe it out. This is a one-man show, a one-person show. I can't command your show for you. I can't script it for you. Script your own show and then nothing can penetrate your integrity; nothing can rob your happiness. As long as you have your last breath you can forgive. If you never forgive the person, you remain a victim of the past for the rest of your life.

Devote yourself to the living principle that nothing bothers you and then, no matter how strong the external forces, you will not be affected. You know your principles well. You are on your personal reality show. Fulfill it by taking action every day and by following this principle.

Great companions wish their partners happiness and wealth. Share this silent joy because your partner is a part of your heaven. If you delete your partner from your heaven, then it is a broken heaven. Your partner is a part of the whole, so you can't cut them out. Dance and do not dance with the devil. Include the devil in your heaven. When you are in a happy place, you leave the devil behind as you leave the room. When you are in line with the principle, it is okay to leave and to not be affected. There is no need to curse because you are not in line with the devil's energy. Every action is in line with the original purpose. An invisible connection exists even if you are ten thousand miles apart.

Respect human differences, be they cultural, behavioral or character. Don't get infected, just respect differences without judgment. The dialectic of self-judgment is judgment of others. Likewise, judgment of others is judgment of self. Always start from the origin, from your heart. Your original spirit is about nurturing and growing, so don't jump into conclusion and judgment. When every person embraces this concept of nurturing and growing, over conclusion and judgment, the world is a much more beautiful place. People interpret religion and philosophy differently, so as to exercise their ego and power. When our safety zone is broken, we use our power to destroy and resent. You can either protect or destroy comfort. Learn to respect the rights of others for an existence of their own choosing. Now there is no revenge; now you can forgive.

Look back into your childhood. Your parents did the best given their capacity, wisdom and intelligence. They did what they thought was right, just as you do what you think is right. Trust people to do their best. Go back and respect that they did their best. Don't take your own malcontent as continuing pain. Many people stay frozen. They blame their parents to justify why they are not happy today. Be happy and respect who you are today. Follow the golden rule and treat people the way you want to be treated. Today, honor your parent's ability. Don't judge or abandon because of their ability; don't mistreat because of their ability.

Chapter 26

I Love Myself

Love is a powerful tool for a successful life. Love yourself to build self-respect. It enables you to have a clear blueprint for your life. Set your life goal, design your life every step of the way. Maintain devotion, dedication and discipline towards your goal of immortality. A journey of ten thousand miles starts with the first step. With self-respect and love of yourself, you will not be attracted to the obstacles of life. You will define your own path, enjoying every step to face any challenge of your life. Life's road does not present a straight path toward immortality. With love and self-respect, you are capable to be united with the universe. With love for self and self-respect, you are able to love the entire world.

Men have dignity and women have respect! When you carry a lack of trust, you separate yourself from others and you become a lonely human being through isolation. Lack of trust makes you vulnerable because it implies that you have possessions that you are afraid of losing. As I asked of you earlier, open your palms and try to grab for a handful of air. The tighter your fists, the less air you have. Open your heart to trust and in return, *Tao* will trust you. Opening your heart to trust and to the nature of *Tao* is to make you a trustworthy individual. In contrast, holding on and lacking trust is the false security of a delusional self. In doing so you strive to possess yourself, yet that is impossible to do. When you pour a cup of coffee into the ocean it is both there and not there. Trust in *Tao* and *Tao* will trust you! To do so, you must let go of your fear of trust. You must ask yourself, "Why do I still have a shield?" A lack of trust is, in fact, a shield that you naively raise to protect yourself. You must maintain innocence to the world. Return to the innocence of a baby! People place so many conditions upon trust, whereas, trust should be unconditional. *Taoist* philosophy is about nurturing one's own spirit and not about worshipping God! Be an extraordinary human and become a dragon!

Some people have a problem with self-worth. Blaring symptoms of a lack of self-worth include thoughts of feeling that you are not worth the time; not worth the compliments; unworthy of gifts; or not worthy of the love of others. When you require that other people prove to you that they are worth it, you also show a lack of self worth. When all other people in the world are stupid and only you are smart, that is a lack of self-worth. You tend to force your value onto others when you are lacking in self-worth. If you have a center of compassion, life should be in balance. When you are your own best friend, then you can be a friend with everyone. When you are your own best friend, then you are not seeking confirmation from others. Why would you want to make another person suffer? If you feel unbalanced, find balance. Find relative balance! Find relative balance from contradiction. There is no ultimate balance, just relative balance. Stupid people look for perfection. Accept yourself as imperfect. If I am shouldering feelings of imperfection, I will try to make others imperfect. It is a compulsive disease! Learn to be your own psychologist. You have to possess great dedication and devotion to find the master within. Dedicate the rest of your life to loving yourself. The power to love your self comes from meditation. As your level of *Qi* rises, so does wisdom. Self-healing is the most powerful healing. Self-healing is the most long lasting healing. Defects and perfection; harmony and balance come through truly accepting yourself with both your defects and your perfections. The small self and the big self are equal to the organic self!

Process # 19: Write twenty ways in which you mistrust yourself! Then forgive yourself. Don't judge your mistrust. Be aware of it, forgive it and drop it.

Be kind today! *Tao* is a combination of both love and hate. The wildflower on the roadside is always prettier than the one at home in the vase. You must learn to enjoy the flower that you have at home. Although the wildflower at the roadside appears to be more exciting and adventurous, everything is based upon your own self-worth. You must understand who you are and what it is that you want. The rat is playing the cat when desire plays you. Be a smart and wise cat so that the rat does not play you. Learn to also appreciate what you don't have. Black can't become white. *Yin* can't be *Yang*! They don't need to be! Look at your fears, know them and deal with them. Have the mercy to love your-self. Take yourself out of the freezer.

You kill a devil by showing the capacity to not even see it as a devil and thus, the capacity to love it. Do not feed a devil with ammunition. Realize that God is in you; *Tao* is within you. Treasure what you have in this moment. Don't sit around in life and wait for the loss of what you have. Regret is a poison inside. Identify the gap and fill up that gap. With each cycle, a hope is born and a truth is lost. Give one hundred percent of what you have and thereby, feel no regret. Never cover your forehead; it is where your spirit resides.

Process # 20: Write a letter to someone. In the letter, express your self-worth.

How do you clear a blockage? The hardest things are overcome by the softest. Water and stillness overcome hardness. Water, though very malleable, overcomes even the hardest rocks with time. Water's quality is softness. Softness and gentleness are applications of *Tao*. Virtue is compassion of *Tao*. The void is the body of *Tao*. Water follows its nature, yet nothing can stop water. Water can carry very large boats and water can flip those boats. Water can bury the boat. Your spirit is the king, but you can kill your spirit. Water is able to carry a boat because of its stillness and quality. If you fight the motion of water, it will flip the boat. You have to work with the motion of water. If you ride the motion of water, then the boat will float.

Instill in your mind that your favorite actor is you. Emotion is a God-given gift to enjoy, but only for three minutes. Don't endlessly persecute yourself with all kinds of emotions, but also be real and don't suppress your emotions. When they continue on for more than three minutes though, then you become pathetic. Then you become self-pitying. When you have an emotion, be like a little child who falls and who looks to see if anyone is looking before he decides whether to cry. Emotions are to be enjoyed for three minutes. After the three minutes come to realize, "Oh! This is no longer fun," and move on. Realize that most people are being pathetic with their-own emotions; they have no time to realize that you are being pathetic also.

Learn to lick your own wounds and then, get up to move on. It feels good to move on. It's a choice. Either you continually wait for someone to come help, or you grow up and move on yourself. Are you growing into heaven or are you going to heaven? When you say, "Going," remember that this is how preachers control you.

Conscience, mercy and forgiveness are the way to love! Conscience gives you the love to deal with forgiveness. Love from the external does not fill the need. You need love from within. Turn the power around. Do not ask, "Do you love me?" Just love yourself! You have everything that you need within you. Look for the visible arrow and look for the invisible arrow. Character and behavior develop over time. One type of invisible arrow is what you bring with you from the long ago past, from the invisible past to the visible now. To solve this, practice good deeds and practice the three treasures of *Tao*—conscience, mercy and forgiveness. Nurture *Jing* and *Qi*, and then you will have a breakthrough!

The reason you see so many clouds is because things have not been resolved.

When you resolve the invisible, then you will understand. The invisible always tries to grab your leg. You know this to be true because repeat patterns keep showing up in your life. We all need to do our due-diligence to find out what blocks us. Fear is also an attachment. Be whole-hearted with your conscience, mercy and forgiveness. The power of the *Tao* is universal. You cannot apply it half-heartedly. *Tao* is a totally selfish *Tao*. Why do you live for others? True compassion does not need to be thought about. Love of humans is different than the love of Tao. My Grand Master *Li* said, "Give up the love of the world and love yourself. Then you begin to build up the love of *Tao*." Follow through with your promise. Saying, "I love you," to others can be a contract. When both want it, it can be broken. The needs that we have are arrows. Curiosity is lethal. It is a need. Your propensity towards curiosity delays the process of deep meditation.

Which would you choose: love from yourself; or a hug from someone whom you would have liked to had a hug from in your childhood? Spiritually, one choice can fix your whole life. It can fix the foundation problem. Cleanse your own mind. Early childhood is the foundation for your entire life. Unfulfilled desires grow up to cripple you, merely because you didn't get something that you desired. An Eastern education delivers very strict guidance. It almost forces success. Western Education does not foster sufficient discipline, but it encourages freedom and passion. Put both together to spell success. You need discipline and love at the same time.

Chapter 27

Play a Damn Good Game

Life is a game of a triangle: the victim, the persecutor and the hero. Everyone in life plays this game in each given moment. Understand the characteristics of each role. Get into and out of the game like a true master. Learn to play the game without attachment to the results of the game. By playing the game with attachment you will suffer from emotion and disease; and this will only decrease the power of the *Yuan Shen,* or original spirit. When you master this game you are able to sign a contract with your own *Yuan Shen.* It is like living with the lotus flower that grows in the mud, all the while presenting it's best to the world. Learn to respect the mud and enjoy the flower. You need the mud to grow the lotus.

When making progress, there are circumstances that can pull on you and suck your energy, situations that pull you to participate in the game. How you react to these situations can cause more emotions and pull you in deeper. Disengage from becoming a victim, a persecutor and a hero. Let a person create drama but disengage yourself from that drama. There is no need for you to participate. Every day, so many events pull on you to participate. You must ask yourself, "Am I willing to participate? Will I play this game?" Remember in the end, to disengage. The game is merely in your own head, "I feel the pain." If you give into even a simple reaction you feed the devil. Negative energy is all he or she wants and needs, just a little, tiny reaction. That is how he or she, the devil gets into you and enslaves you.

Appreciate everything, every day, regardless of whether you perceive it as beautiful or ugly. This is the dialectic of life. Don't possess anything. Don't even possess the concept that the purpose of life is to be happy. Whether it's victim, prosecutor, or hero, see the dialectic in playing each of the three roles! Then, you will understand how each role, plays into the other.

Have a goal of entertaining and enjoying life. How can you be the hero of your own life? You do so by entertaining life and not being entertained by life. If you have a mind and soul, then you have enough to be a healer in life. Know the game and master the game. Play a good damn game! Don't be under the illusion that goal setting comes without a cost. Find the faith and courage to follow up to *Tao*. *Tao* begins with one; one becomes two; two becomes three; three becomes ten thousand.

Life is endlessly entertaining; so do not limit your dragon. Feel the movement, see the movement and be the dragon. You victimize your character because you think that you should be another character. If that is what you want, then pretend and get into a new character. When you were a child you had an endless power of imagination. As an adult you have to re-learn to be a dragon. The way to ride a dragon is to learn to be the dragon.

The chessboard is not life. It teaches you to follow the rules. Moving the chess pieces is, in part, luck. You create the move; then you create the luck. You create your own luck. If you continue to play by the same rules, then you will continue to get the same results. If you continue to see yourself as a garbage man, so to speak, then you will continue to be the garbage man. You must walk the talk.

Practice your game face by developing a strategy. Pretend you are going to a second-life city to shop through all the costumes that are available. Use your five senses to create a new life. You do not have the right to refuse this gift of a new life from God. The game requires one hundred percent dedication, devotion and discipline. The key to success is dedication, devotion and discipline. The seed of the plant requires nurturing so don't take your eyes off the process. The game involves going to several different places and envisioning your new costume, or new life in that location.

Process # 21: Develop your new costume by visiting the following four locations in your meditation:

1. Visit a large city. You are in the middle of a large city. The city represents your mature, professional life along

with your prosperity and accomplishments. See yourself in this city. What does it look like, feel like and smell like?

2. Next, visit you current home. It represents your spiritual life and how well you are connected with the spirit.

3. Third, visit a mountain, there you cultivate and convert wisdom with which you return to essential nature and stillness.

4. Finally, visit your home growing up. It represents the power to go back and change, to transform the power of wisdom to make change in your life and to return to the womb.

Returning to the original self is the nature of *Tao*. Every day is a triangle game. Always exercise your brain and never lose your passion for life. You must maintain passion for life so that you don't persecute others by giving up on yourself. It is then that you become someone else. You must know your spiritual and personal identity; never let go of it. Translate these principles into application. In being strong, it is okay to allow yourself to be weak. If you want to live in an illusion, then you will be in a life of illusions all the time. You have been taught the techniques. Now it is up to you to implement them. Try to catch yourself judging. You are only hurting yourself by judging others. These techniques only work if you have compassion, mercy and forgiveness. If you win, then everybody wins! Develop three-dimensional observation. You have to kiss yourself and whomever you may talk about. Small talk can really be big talk. Through invisible signs, you see the principle. All humans have passion for life. If both people win, then there is creation and grand harmony. Work your triangle goal every day. It's about getting the persecutor, hero, and victim out of the game.

In the triangle game each person has a preference and a choice for how to play and what role to choose. Each person plays a role, and then justifies that role through their logical mind, or logical culture. The government, for instance, may attack or impose its beliefs on other countries and then justify it through their eyes. There is, however, always a return action. Return is the motion of *Tao*. The victim feels justified in retaliating against the persecutor and in the process becomes the persecutor. The persecutor then becomes the victim, and the hero judges the victim and persecutor as lesser and in need of help. The hero becomes hated and will create victims and persecutors. This game goes on all the time; we unconsciously rotate through the three positions. When you experience emotion, what role do you play? As long as you are a material human, then you cannot get away from this game. It is part of the basic reality of this material world. Once you understand that this is the logic and the game, you had better become a master of it and play a good damn game!

When your mind sets free from logic, judgment stops. Judgment is simply the victim, hero and persecutor recycling. When you become really smart, you don't kick the soccer ball at the wall haphazardly. You choose whether to be a victim or not. So don't choose it and you won't be a victim! This is the triangle game of life.

Suppose that something happens and you are the recipient victim. Do you say, "This happened to me," or did it just happen? Being a victim means that you put a charge on it. "This happened to me." When you are the victim you will attack the persecutor, and then the victim switches to become the hero. You can play all the roles and we all do. There is a constant bouncing effect off each other. Playing the good damn game is when you don't play. All these positions are choices. Take attention away from the positions and get yourself out. You are none of them. Nothing is happening to you. The drama has nothing to do with you, unless you choose that.

Every position you play is based upon the logical sense of your intelligence to play a certain role. To play a persecutor, you have the law or rules behind you. What's right and what's wrong? You have your own reasons—religion, culture, power and control—which are based on your own logic to measure the world. The persecutor thinks that he has every right to enforce, to interfere. By doing this, the persecutor turns into the hero. However, as stated, there is always a bounce, a return. The persecutor will be persecuted. A persecutor gives birth to a victim. When you make a victim, you also make them the persecutor. Heroes have justice in the mind, but they enforce justice with force, so they become the persecutor and make victims.

Understand that this game is going on all the time. Every single day of your life journey, you rotate into each position again and again. When you experience emotion, you experience one of these roles. As long as you remain on this earth as a material human, you cannot avoid this game. This is a basic human reality in the logical world. You are automatically enrolled. Once you understand this as a game, you are in the logic of it. Now play the game well.

The warrior must hold the three treasures of *Tao*: consciousness, mercy and forgiveness. When you play the roles of the triangle game, you need to apply the treasures of *Tao*. The hero needs to display conscience and mercy. A persecutor requires conscience and a victim applies forgiveness. Have no attachment, because conscience, mercy and forgiveness will keep you from attaching. Then what? There is no more game to play! This is what immortality is about.

The ground is dusty, it's ordinary, but those who have conscience all of a sudden become extraordinary humans and are able to stand in the clouds. Because you have mercy, you are like a God and feel the pain of humanity. With conscience, you have come from humanity. You understand and wish them well. Mercy enables you to stand on the clouds and never fall. Forgiveness, like wings, helps you to fly. Without forgiveness you can't move, there is no action. Forgiveness provides the power for you to fly. Forgiveness provides action. You can only ride the hidden dragon if you have the three treasures. Without them you cannot ride. You must be disciplined, devoted to your true self and dedicated to stick to the dragon. Never compromise your true integrity. Other people are not accountable to you. When you hold others accountable, you persecute, you escape responsibility and you fool yourself.

A relationship is companionship. If you feel companionship with yourself, then you can have a relationship. You don't have to get infected. Let your partner be who he or she is. People maintain their own role. In some relationships, love becomes harassment; love becomes hate and love becomes a dictatorship. You are not obligated to walk into that model. There is no need to get infected by that. Do not take the guilt. Do not allow your love to become rape. Do not say, "She prevents me from doing what I want to do." When two people get together, the relationship is a sacred bond. If it's sacred, it deserves to be honored. You don't know how long the relationship will last, so honor it in this moment. You must learn to honor a relationship to the best of your ability. Be who you are and what you believe, but show honor in your relationship. When you are done in a relationship, disengage with peace. The ultimate peace is to walk away without guilt. If you feel guilty then you are not ready. Then you are still playing the game.

Chapter 28

Moon on the Treetop

When you see the moon on the treetop during a full moon what do you see? There is so much attachment in life, detouring you from your goal—see and not see. My master said that when you are at the stillness moment, you cling to break through *Tao*. You must be a fool. Stillness is the root of *Tao* and the void is the body of *Tao*. Softness is the application of *Tao* and virtue is the compassion of *Tao*. The mind and intent stay in stillness, leading you to brightness and enlightenment. We often see a small part of the mystical dragon. We can't bring the words to describe this true quality of joy. Great photographers can hold the true beauty in their heart forever without using the camera. True enlightenment to *Tao* is the same. The moment is fleeting;

if you try to grasp it, it is gone. See without seeing; know without knowing. Create your own heaven. Life is a dream! The empty circle with a dot in the center is the Chinese character for the sun! The heart is bright in hope and light. You don't need to retire; you just need to change your attitude. Be absolutely certain that you can create multiple lives. It is all based upon stillness, love and mercy. Never let go of your vision and goal. You can attach, detach, rebirth and create. Exercise the will of your power. You have to trust the will of power. I can do it! I am master of my own!

"Bright moon hanging in blue sky and blue water;

Taming the tiger and dragon in the spine of the rocky mountain.

The lazy clouds hang over the tranquil mountain.

Mountain deer playfully roam the fields of snow.[1]

A mystical vapor rises from the cauldron in the lonely cave,

Cultivating three treasures on the road to tranquility.

The mother of *Wu Ji* gathers *Xing* and *Ming*.

The mystical warrior is taming the poisons,

Returning to the heavenly palace and singing the heavenly song."

The mystical gateway is always in front of you. How

---

[1] this describes achievement of body, mind and spirit

many fools do not awake from their dream? If you are a fool you let things distract you from the things that you need to see. You dance around the issues rather than deal with them. What things appear to be may, in fact, not be what they are. Life is a collection of pieces that, when put together, make you whole. Do not dance around the concept, or you will make the void full. We are chasing, judging, being judged; always covering up what life is supposed to be. If you have the will to be dialectical it doesn't matter what is in front of you. It is how you appreciate and enjoy it. Honor your own things to do. It is not for me to judge, only to watch my own spirit perform. Do not vigorously defend concepts. Look into the eyes and do not judge self, do not judge others. If you vigorously defend, it is yourself that you hold onto. It may look very real, but non-being is the objective. If you think that you have broken through, then you have just fallen into another trap. Be humble!

What you don't want to hear, you sometimes have to hear. Exercise the options! We all have the option not to live. When food goes through the intestine it becomes excrement, but Buddha, God or *Tao* is still in my heart. That is your choice. You must deal with the fear of death. See and not see, know and not know. If you truly believe this then you must be willing to play your best. Play your best violin. Sink these notes into your soul. Life comes before possessions! If you always worry that you can't afford it, you will never afford it. You have to take the joy instead of pain and guilt. It is not, "Am I worth it?" Instead, "Is it worth it?" "I can always buy it," is a statement of self-doubt. If it is important in your life, then just do it. Change the poor mindset. Live like a billionaire. See yourself as a spiritual billionaire. If you don't exercise the power of the will you will never get what you want. Dream big! I see it, I want it, I deserve it! I grow into heaven.

Every day is a heavenly day. If you don't look at it as a heavenly day, then it can be a hell day. Life is a living hell? Life is not a living hell; it is a living heaven. When God brings more, you don't thank more. You thank in your all in every moment. You always appreciate with one hundred percent. Sometimes you hear, sometimes you don't. Every day is a heavenly day; every day is an appreciative day.

Chapter 29

Can You See Yourself Without a Mirror?

This phenomenal question is the question that I had to face for ten years while in the mountain as a priest. Every single time I failed and got a bamboo on the butt! I tried with all my intelligence to answer that question. Every time I experienced the invisible bamboo on my butt. My master taught me not to use the human intelligence but to believe in *Taoist* wisdom. Let go of the attachment to self and the universe. Surrender yourself to the void. Surrender yourself to the universe and your body will become the most magical laboratory of the universe; knowing the world without stepping out of your room. Do you truly understand the meaning of doing nothing and leaving nothing undone? Just as you and the universe mirror each other, so do you and your *Yuan Shen.*

Process # 22: At the end of one year ask this same question and give your answer. Can you see yourself without a mirror?

There are always options in life; there are always choices. Master *Li* said, "If you don't have the strength to look at the ugly, how can you know beauty?" She did not try to raise the boat; she just added water. The knife is not dangerous; it is your mind that is dangerous. Do not persecute the material; more willingly, work on your mind. Life is a dream. When you wake from a dream, you realize everything is empty. Choose to nurture spirit as opposed to nurturing a dream.

Chuang Tsu wrote: "Once upon a time, I, *Chuang Tsu,* dreamed I was a butterfly flying happily here and there, enjoying life without knowing who I was. Suddenly I woke up and I was indeed *Chuang Tsu*. Did *Chuang Tsu* dream he was a butterfly or did the butterfly dream he was *Chuang Tsu*?"[2]

He can't figure out whether he is the butterfly or the butterfly is he. Why try to figure it out? Become immortal! Be real and don't fantasize about a concept of what you think an

---

[2] Chuang Tsu, Inner Chapters, translated by Gia-Fu Feng and Jane

English, Amber Lotus Publi*Sh*ing, San Francisco, 1974, pg. 48

immortal should be like. Feel the energy of life. Don't persecute the present energy. If you are feeling sad, honor that feeling for three minutes and then in the fourth minute, let the feeling go. Ride the energy, feel the dragon, and then balance it. Be truthful about your emotions. Feel your heart first and don't be so busy trying to feel good. If you can't be ordinary, then you can't be extraordinary.

Can you see yourself without a mirror? It depends on whether you want to see yourself or not. If you don't then the answer is no. If you do want to see yourself without a mirror, then the answer is yes. There are ten thousand answers to this question. Who is the self? This question is about the third side of the coin. It's about the process. There is a lot behind you, who you are, what you are and when you are. Seeing is equal to how you see, when you see, where you see; zero, one, two, three or ten thousand. Mirror, why is mirror, what is mirror? There is too much "monkey" mind in trying to answer this question. The whole question is a dragon. You can touch one part of the dragon but is that the whole dragon? Is the butterfly you or are you the butterfly? Identify self, identify your dragon and stick with that dragon. Identify the feel of the dragon and then let go of it. For every desire there is manifestation. For every lack of desire there is mystery. It just It!

Ask, "Will I ride the dragon?" Then sit on the dragon. Feel the ride of the dragon. Let go of the dragon. Reach immortality. *Tao* is not answerable. If it is describable, then it is not *Tao*. By the same token, if you say that *Tao* is indescribable then you have described *Tao*.

We always want to understand in order to be secure. Logic, however, creates confusion. Logic blinds us, leading to a dead end. No matter who is there, just be yourself one hundred percent. A master musician is asked to play music, but when he arrives there is only a piano and a cow, there is no audience. What does he do? Play the music! The greatest people are those who self entertain and maintain joy within. A master musician is a master musician regardless of who the audience is. He plays for himself and not the audience. A true dragon doesn't care where it goes.

Life is fun; use the dialectical. Honor your heart, then you won't age so fast. Be a perfect bridge with joyful living; don't worry about the next day. Wherever life could lead tomorrow, you don't need to worry, or see. Today, live under the principle of integrity. The fundamental philosophy of your own true heart is to live today. You don't have to get infected, or live in fear of tomorrow. Live to function today. In the moment! Then, should you find yourself falling from the sky, before you end your physical life, you just say, "Now I know how to fly."

With the right attitude, you live all your life with what you believe, that is instantaneous enlightenment. What do I do with it, how can I be wiser, how can I continue observing and absorbing without judging? When you catch yourself, immediately make a statement from the heart instead of reacting from the head. Trust your heart! Otherwise, whose heart do you trust? You set yourself a trap by walking in a fantasy world created by others. You prevent yourself from walking with God. Women, learn to be more logical. Men, learn what you don't have. Prevent yourself from projecting a fake model. Taking non-action is taking action. If you want people whom you wish for in dreams, then live your dream. Project an invisible influence, a peaceful revolution, by teaching without words and doing without work. This concept is understood by very few. Affect people's lives by living, through example, a life of quality and integrity. Others will see and follow you. The *Tai Chi* principle is effortless. You are not here to force others, maybe herd them a little with guidance.

Can you see yourself without a mirror? If you can see the mirror, then there is a need for the mirror, a need to see yourself ugly or beautiful. One day, you decide you don't need a mirror, so there is no longer a mirror. "Ever desire less one can see the mystery, ever desiring one sees the manifestations".[3] What kind of manifestation? Is it logical or illogical? It does come both ways, but you often have a string attached to your wish, to your desire, so it's logical. You are your own manifestation. Do you know that? We are the manifestation of God. If there is a desire, there is always a product so you can desire. My Master *Li* asks, "Can you see yourself without a mirror?" Everyday finds its own mystery. Every day has its exciting answer.

---

[3] *Tao Te Ching,* Translated by Gia-Fu Feng and Jane English, 1972, Alfred A. Knopf, New York,. Pg. 3

Chapter 30

Let Go of the Mask

Life is a play, let go of the mask. We often present a mask to the world, living in the insecure and illusionary world of self and others. The mask has misled you and has destroyed your true nature. *Tao* gives a gift of choice. We should make the choice of the true self and not the self of illusion. Be brave and be loyal to your true self. Enjoy and entertain the mask of your choice without attaching to it. As my Master used to say, "When you are facing the most painful moments in life, allow yourself to cry for three minutes and then return back to the natural." Do not pretend or escape from the reality of life. Life is just a simple, joyful play or game.

Don't wear other people's shoes! Don't wear Reuben's shoes if you are Allen. Respect your own gifts and be true to them. Ask yourself honestly, "What is my true gift?" Can you be honest, will you respect this gift or will you force it out of your life? Mothers and fathers oftentimes unintentionally force their children away from their true gifts. Children are frequently forced to wear a "costume" that is very ugly. Wearing this costume brings up emotions of regret. As a child, you may not have had the power to make your own choices. Your parents may have cast choices upon you. As an adult, you are now well capable to decide what shoes fit your feet. Too often, during life, we give away our true love, compromising our integrity for something we dislike. You are no longer the child of your parents. Now you are capable of making change. Have no regrets. Wear your own shoes. Return to your true self and don't compromise self-integrity.

Process # 23: Determine what your true gifts are. What are your true talents? What is your true love? Be honest with yourself in answering these questions. Find your essential nature!

You must become a good human before you can be a super human. Respect intelligence and the spirit. Raise your level of *Qi* and the spirit will rise. Are you in life to destroy others, or to balance yourself? There are no opponents in life. Your success is not dependent upon another's failure. In life you have to learn to respect yourself by learning to lose. Losing is not losing per se, it is learning about yourself.

Process # 24: List all the dialectical relations you have learned.

There was once a businessman on a boat who had a gold belt wrapped around his waist. He used the gold to conduct business but it weighed him down. A storm blew up and the flipped the boat. He was reluctant to give up the gold belt, but he would lose his life by holding onto it. Will you hold onto the gold? Will you hold onto the material and lose your life? For sure, a beginning is to not lose this moment, no matter what. This is a start, but do not stop there. If you stop here, then you will have a long way to go.

Process # 25: Bake a basket of cookies and give the cookies individually to a number of people. Within thirty seconds of talking with a person you must give them a cookie. You must give a cookie to every person you talk with.

There is one way to hell but ten thousand ways to heaven. Join the play as if you were a permanent member of the Broadway show. There is no pain! No person can ever cause a loss in your life if you play by different rules. Being a member of your Broadway cast, staying with true dedication is the most important rule to follow. Once you master the game, you master the rules. When you are rigid about your character you have lost the ability to be the dragon. Don't judge! When you are rigid, you will vigorously defend your character. That is how the rat plays the cat, rather than the cat playing the rat.

Make a contract with God, "I will take the mask off at the end of the day." Spirits can only be greatly nourished in the dream. Meditation is a knock at the door. When you awake, your mind is busy all day long. Allow yourself to play with your accessories during the day. Take the accessories off when you sleep. Meditate to wake up spirit and to be nourished. Meditation is active regulation of the spirit. Sleep without meditation is passive nourishment. Nourish the spirit with self-regulated sleep. When meditating, all systems shut down to nourish the spirit actively. One good hour of good meditation is worth five hours of sleep.

The point is you must be willing to let go and to know yourself. You don't have to possess the moment. Beauty can be the only sword in the soul. Use that sword wisely and don't abuse and become a fool of it. If you document it, it will become your own invisible sword over your head. The sword's drop tames emotions inside, so you must learn to use it. See what is there and not what you want to see. You don't have to choose the devil within yourself. You can choose God. God is within. The more you dance with the devil, the more you become the devil. Watch out for the sugarcoated bullet. Always watch for the sugarcoated canon ball. It can not only kill you, but also kill everybody who is with you. Do things with dignity and respect. A principle is something you can defend with your soul. Ask yourself if you feel good about it and be real in your answer. It's a challenge to stop judging others. It's also a challenge to not enjoy a challenge. Every time you judge, you dig a hole in your own heart. If you truly learn dialectical thinking you are an old, peaceful soul in a young body. On the other hand, if you dance with the devil you become the devil.

Chapter 31

Finding Unity from Contradiction
the Coin Has Two Sides

Things always have two sides: beautiful and ugly, motion and still, happy and sad, white and black, past and future. These two sides are the unit of the one whole. Through comparison, to identify one or the other, there is a difference between humans and God. God does not see two sides. Humans see a difference while God sees the unity and beyond. We see the world with intelligence. God sees the world with compassion and love. *Ying* and *Yang* is the unity of *Tao*. My Master told me that when a musician plays to a cow, without appreciation of the cow, he is not a musician but just an ordinary man. You can't separate yourself from the world. Loving and respecting your enemy is equal to loving and respecting yourself. Balance and harmony is the true purpose of life. We seek unity from contradiction rather than finding disunity. Enlightening the devil in you to see love is better, in every way, than trying to kill the devil. Enlightening the devil to find the light within is more powerful than any technique to kill the devil.

Whenever you take a side on an issue, without being aware of it, you are already in trouble. Look dialectically to see both sides. Emit *Qi* to dissolve blocks, germs and virus. Balance the germ and it vanishes. Balance the argument and it vanishes. Once again, you must have a passion for solving the puzzle to balance and return to *Tao*. Balance and vanish! Don't get hung up on results, walk away without taking credit. Before you take action, be still to listen to the body. Look inside! When you return to the stillness and become quiet, often an issue disperses. Do not label things; it is merely *Tao* giving opportunity for internal reflection.

A coin has three sides, but if you can't find the second side, then surely you will never find the third side. Do not attach yourself to a concept. Something that you possess can eventually possess you if you are not careful. Give the freedom of love, space. Do not attach judgments. Do not place your love into concepts, lest you destroy your beliefs about your love. The principle is not the absolute truth. Even *Taoist* principle is not the absolute. That which can be described is not *Tao*.

A man's tears are worth more than gold. A man needs to learn how to cry, while the woman needs to learn to smile. Women tend to love "Love." They love affection and love to feel valued. Men and woman share the world, women (*Yin*) own fifty percent and men (*Yang*) own fifty percent. Don't pretend to be immortal, be human! Only when you are not in control are you in control. There is the rat, the cat and the rat-cat relationship. The merging of the two is the third side of the coin, the dialectical side.

Live knowing that tomorrow is a mystery. Accept that you have more to learn and more to understand. Every judgment is simply a reflection of memory. Judgments change as your individual understanding grows. Judgment is based upon knowledge of the moment. It is based upon past experience and past intelligence, regardless of how flawed that experience or intelligence may be. Be wise to understand that every thought and every judgment is merely an entertainment of the past.

We are so confused about the unknown that we pretend to know. It is okay to respect your knowledge of the past, but remember that it is based upon your understanding at that time. Are you the entertainer of life, or is life entertaining you? What do you choose? Life doesn't go by what we want. Entertain and look beyond. Look and live in both dimensions and then live in the third dimension. Live beyond the spiritual and material realms. Live in the place of the hidden dragon. Again, *Tao* is an interesting concept. The more you think you get it, the more you lose it. You cannot describe it. You can only feel it and when you think you can feel it, that's when you lose it.

The dialectical is that you're right and I'm right too; it's just the way we look at it. Many things in life look spiritual but they are not. You need to create your own definitions. Truth always finds its own way to be revealed. You can't cover up the truth. Master *Li* instructed me, "Open your palm. Now cover the sky for me." You can't do it. The truth can't be hidden. Never try to fool a human spirit. Every human spirit deserves dignity and respect.

Imagine that you are brought blindfolded into a dark room, and that eight people are in the room throwing rocks at you. How do you not get hit? Don't go into logic. How do you not get hit? Kill yourself first. Ask, "What rock? I don't see a rock." When you go into the logic you create a paper tiger. You become bigger and bigger, and so you become an easier target. You need to be able to get into the zone and only then are you able to avoid it. You must go into the mode of self and selflessness, then merge and look beyond. Only then can you come out alive. Denying your fear, denying your environment and trying to figure it out logically makes you become vulnerable. So, the best thing to do is to give up all intelligence. Live in the total illogic. When you are in the zone, you have no reflection. Intelligence will tell you how to avoid, how to be afraid. But the illogic will allow you to not be seen anymore. Diminish your presence and you are gone.

God created the devil. The devil is the darkness. This is dialectical. One doesn't exist without the other. To get rid of the devil, be in the light. Keep your eye on the goal. Keep the attention on the little spot in the darkness. The light will grow. Get the devil to realize that it has a light inside. Tell the devil, "You are the God." This is the kindness. Every human is born with kindness. Confucius says, "The beginning of human nature is kindness." As we grow up it gets lost. It's like the diamond covered by the mud. You just polish it up to see it.

"Who called you the devil? You are God!" There is no force needed to convert. Violence and force are what the devil needs to exist. Be in kindness and you help him to see. Bring the light and life into a human's life. This is nature. Merge both of them. Observe them and understand them without attachment. Respect and honor them for who they are.

God and the devil are just two sides of human nature. Religion twists it and makes them a tangible concept. No! When the *Tao* rises one inch, the devil rises one foot. It takes much effort for the *Tao* to rise one inch, but very little to go far into devilish tendencies. It's a lot of hard, challenging work to gain a little wisdom. Wisdom comes from all the darkness. It's like a flower that must rise above the mud. Take the nutrients from the mud and rise above it. Absolutely stay firm with what you understand is your life purpose. Then, when you see God, you see the devil and you embrace them all. When approaching life from *Tao,* ten cattle can't draw you to turn your head back. Once you truly understand *Tao,* you will be good at everything. *Tao* runs through everything. Once you understand the *Yin* and the *Yang* then you can see the third dimension and beyond.

Be like R2D2 from Star Wars when he projects an image. Your spirit does this. Allow the spirit to show you, to project the image and to show you the way. If you use your logic, you cannot understand what your spirit says. Lose control so that you can let illogic dominate, then you will be able to see and understand the wisdom. This is how you feel your spirit, feel your Master. You must be willing to let go of your presence, let go of your identity as a human. Spirit functions in a very illogical way. It functions without form. You must cross over a boundary to get there. How do you cross over this boundary?

From a solid "I" to an invisible "I," all you need to do is destroy logic. Then, you are able to translate the language, to live in the same frequency. Spirit is always able to access you, but you are not merging with spirit. You block the spirit and it's upon you to open the communication. You must be willing. Willingness allows you to find the hidden dragon. Only then can you ride the dragon and function as the illogical world does. Then, you are the One. When you are the one, you can hear, sense, know, do and experience the power and the joy of spirit. When you lose control, you will know yourself. You are a twenty-four hour spirit. In order to access spirit, actively provide an inviting condition. Access the Master Within by cleansing, balancing and letting go of emotions.

Lao Tsu was the first to speak of dialectical thinking. In the West it was Hegel. People do not understand in bits and pieces. This is why I pack into this book ten years of training in the temple, four years of college and five thousand years of Taoist knowledge, all downloaded into this book. When you trust yourself enough, when you have good guides to teach you to not believe in the logic, the possibilities are endless. Logical thinking is a poison deep inside your soul. What logic? Logic is based upon your limited understanding at that time. It carries such a deep influence. It will make you compromise your integrity again and again. Don't underestimate your spirit power. When you feel a lack of ability to dream, take a wild leap to be on God's side. Believe that you have superpowers in you to guide you out of the darkness and out of the confusion.

When you see a beggar on the street, what do you see and what do you feel? What goes through your mind and what do you do? When we see things, your logical mind is immediately activated and you start judging the situation or person. Is it real or not real? Should I give or not give? If begging for food, I'll give food. This is a lot of logic. This is years of information. It's not about that moment. So when it comes to activate logic, some are quick with reflection and some slower. You are passionately giving, but it's not returned. So what happens? Destroy these concepts.

Religious values make you a victim of your own religious belief. I add a disclaimer here! I am not trying to convert you to Taoism and I'm not telling you to abandon other religions. I am just offering you my opinions. I am here to entertain myself. You are in my world. So many things become an invisible lock on yourself; religion, culture, job, schooling and upbringing. What's pathetic about this is, we all volunteer to be locked up. The devil has you! We are all volunteering to embrace the devil. Okay, so entertain him for three minutes, but only three minutes.

You volunteer your integrity and spirit to be put into a cage and then you turn around and beg God to free you. This is disingenuous prayer. You have asked to be caged. In order to reunite with your own spirit you need to learn to synchronize your spirit with your body. "How," you ask? Let go! Whatever it is that you deal with, what you really ought to do is to let go of the need. Curiosity is a bullet to your heart. If you can admit your needs are an illusion, then you are one step closer to *Tao*. The true learning of *Tao* is invisible, illogical learning. It cannot be spoken. Once it's spoken it becomes logic. We speak to learn, but understand that *Tao* cannot be spoken. This, my friend, is dialectical!

You can operate in all dimensions; the mind, body and spirit functioning all together in full capacity, logically and illogically. It is not just the material success; it's the spiritual success too. All habits, all behavior, all patterns of thinking, all ways of logical recognition of the world break loose. Be willing to change and then take the action to change. When you are totally exhausted you function better, because the logic becomes less strong. You experience what we call, "Taoist hallucination" and in that hallucination, you start to see your own spirit. That is why, when you are very tired, you sometimes become giddy and silly. That is spirit taking over after intelligence has exhausted itself. Are you in a dream or is the dream in you?

Sweetness comes after bitterness. You can't know sweetness without bitterness. Truth hurts but the pain of it only lasts for three minutes. Always look for the other side of "me." Believe your logic; don't deny your logic, but believe more in the illogic. Envision first and then backtrack to fill in the steps to get there. Always find your twin soul. When you are in logic, find the illogical and when you are in the illogical, then find the logic. When you can cross the boundary with ease, you have unlimited opportunity.

Dialectic is a philosophical concept that allows you to understand that black and white are the third side of the coin merging. It is seeing a new product come out from individual products, another, invisible product. It is producing other realities—multidimensional realities. Discover the invisible energy from the merging of the two sides of the visible, then, create a new realm.

Go into your heart to produce a practical, realistic, full-of-joy-and-happiness model that you can use for your entire life. Give up the ten thousand models to create and merge into a new model. Merging the two creates the third side of the coin, the visible and invisible model of *Tao*. See and not see, do and not do. Do not persecute either side; it just it. Ask how to ride it? Life is a frequency flow. It is how to be a master of your own life, by understanding the merging of the two forces into your life. *Tai Chi* is the physical application of a dialectical philosophy. Soft and hard together to produce *Tai Chi*—the third side is the connection to Tao.

Chapter 32

Follow What Is Nature

There is no true path! There is no pre-designed path when water flows down the mountain. Water flows with one intent and that is towards where it is designed to flow, a place of balance. Understand your own limits in your character so that you will always be able to smile at the end. When you follow and exercise your ego you wrestle with God. How would you escape from a whirlpool in the ocean? Take a deep breath and let yourself be pulled down. Then find a path toward a new, less turbulent place. When you are in a canoe on a rough ocean, how would you make the best of your time? Following what is your own nature will bring you joy and happiness. Your life will be filled with success and happiness in each given moment.

Sit in the middle of a busy road and know that you are soaking in the tranquility of a remote mountaintop. When you experience the taste of a great apple, you can't wait to share the joy of that taste. Get out of the way and let *Tao* come through. Don't condemn your wounded self. It is the best that you have until the essential self shines through. It is your spirituality! It is not a place; it's a moment.

Have you taken the time to know yourself? You have to be very patient to know yourself. If you are not patient enough, you may only hate yourself. Unless you are dialectical, you tend to see ugliness rather than beauty. You have to take the time to truly see yourself, know both sides of yourself. Your essential nature is your mirror. The question becomes whether you are ready to see what is being reflected. Reflect nothing but the truth. Pre-heaven spirit knows not to punish the post-heaven spirit. Is the post heaven spirit ready, or open to see what is being reflected. The essential nature reflects very clearly. You have to be able to put the puzzle together though. Don't punish yourself. Instead, harmonize yourself. Be patient, compassionate, merciful and forgiving. Continue to practice so that you can know what you need a mirror for. My heart is not my mirror. Rather my mirror is my heart. There is no sweeping to do. If you still have something to work for, then how can you become Buddha? When there is no dust in the mirror then there is no mirror.

It is a lonely journey to the cave. On the way, I pass a bridge over a mountain river. On the way back, I again pass the bridge over the mountain river. Yet, they are no longer the mountain, the bridge or the river. I am no longer myself. This is a principle. Of course, physically they are still a mountain, a bridge and a river. I am no longer who I was yet I am still "me." Every concept is a trap. Can you see yourself without a mirror? Taoism uses poems to express the dialectic principles of *Tao*. It also uses poems to express alchemy. First "I," second "I," third "I," fourth "I," and fifth "I," there are five dimensions in "I." Post heaven I, Pre-heaven I, the third I is the beginning of the immortal. The void becomes the body of the fourth I. The void returns to *Tao*, which is the true I, the immortal fifth I.

Watch and hear your words. Listen very carefully to what you say. Be the best listener of your own self. If you can always listen to yourself you will always win. If against an opponent, then you will not show any weakness. If you have a self-esteem problem, then you talk to make others believe that you know something. If you have to enforce what it is you say, then already you have a weak foundation on which to build. Listen, do not engage and talk. If you learn this concept you can always find out who is your true friend. True friends never have to cover their heart. If you don't trust yourself, then I don't trust you and God doesn't trust you. There are many scenarios about trust. If you don't trust, then you have to ask why. When you say, "I can't trust you" you are saying, "I can't trust myself." Always say the same sentence and listen. If there is no target, whom are you speaking to?

When you say, "I want to stop" if you really mean that, then there is no need to say you want to stop, you just stop.

Likely you are saying that you want to stop to solicit responses and approval from others. You must become your own best friend. Tell yourself repeatedly, "I can do it. I can do it!" I become my best buddy of my own spirit. You can't merely say, "Help," instead you have to help yourself. Be willing to kiss yourself and to hug yourself. You are your own soul mate. The statement "I am looking for my soul mate" becomes, "I am my own soul mate." Have faith in yourself. When you ask the question, "Why can't God see me?" it is because you don't see yourself. To ensure your gift from God, you don't ask God for a gift only to not appreciate it. Be thankful for all the gifts that you receive. Don't put conditions on a gift. We are our own gift. A crisis is opportunity and opportunity is a crisis.

Every day, you must exercise your will power. Every day, you must sharpen your sword. You will never be powerful physically, mentally or spiritually unless you exercise. To follow is wisdom. Don't judge the sentence, more willingly, judge the intent. Take the time to know yourself first before you begin to make all sorts of decisions in exerting your willpower. The good masters always catch the student's tail at the right time. Sometimes the door to heaven can only be unlocked three times. So do not keep yourself out by continually locking the door. Find your will power to be brave and truthful. When you speak about problems, it doesn't make you a bad person. It doesn't necessarily mean that you are using it as an excuse. Take the right action at the right moment with the right attitude.

Do you really know who you are? "I am who I am!" You must truly know yourself to successfully deal with people. If you don't know who you are, then you have self-doubt and you begin to question. You must know that you have the right to exist. "I am the master of my own and I can do it." Darkness is the gateway to the mystery. Coming out of the gateway is also a mystery, gateway of the womb. Nurture in the unknown. When you see the devil you become the devil, so don't see the devil. Challenge represents happiness and making choices. The first treasure of *Tao* is conscience and then mercy. It is always up to you to make choices. When the most feared moment arises, you are choosing between yourself or *Tao*. If you try to confront the devil, you will become the devil. Playing no game is in fact playing a game. Face people compassionately. Face them with conscience, mercy and forgiveness. If you have these qualities, you will always make the right choice. Remember, mercy is a gift from God. You are always able to remember the goodness and the light. Make sure that you stick with the dragon. Make no judgment of performance. It is the process that matters.

You must retain relative balance between logical and illogical. Find balance from the contradiction. There is no ultimate balance. For that reason, you find your own balance. *Ying/Yang*, how many forms and shapes come when the symbol starts turning? Millions! But no matter how many forms, they always retain relative balance. This is how the universe has functioned for hundreds of millions of years. The past, future and present of your life should already retain relative balance. So there is no need to suffer from the past or fear of the future. Just enjoy the present. "It just it!" This is the true hidden dragon.

You must have an unconditionally open heart to receive. If you decide to open, in that case open entirely! Don't put conditions upon it. Conditional love doesn't get you anywhere. The process is to give, receive and appreciate everything. If you trust, trust in *Tao* and at that time *Tao* will trust you back. My Master *Li* says, "Trust is illogical, but of course it comes with the logical." When you get there, it really becomes illogic. So, really trust in *Tao* and detach from *Tao*. Or else, if you don't detach, you are merely looking for another confirmation from *Tao*. You become persecutor of *Tao*. Never negotiate; never blame. Just know *Tao* will trust you back.

When energy stands out, it can only attract the same kind of energy. You don't have to pick and choose, or worry about attracting the wrong energy. This is the secret to building community around you. This is making a *Qi* social club. You attract the same frequency into your community. When you ask, "Why do I always attract jerks?" now you know why. Cleanse your own soul and then send out your energy, the energy that you want returned. A soul mate should find you, not you find him, or her. You put out your illogical energy and he becomes attracted logically to you.

Your husband or wife is only a companion; the journey is alone. Look beyond and not just to the present moment. You have a choice. Do not put your life's control into someone else's hands. Anything that does not serve your immortal path is from post-heaven. Women look for men to balance and men look for women to balance. Girls connect to the father and boys to the mother. Whatever is missing is what we always look for in life. We sometimes find a partner to balance previous generations. The outside is a mirror of the inside. You can see your frequency and pattern. You are born into this world forgetting how powerful you are. Human nature is to try to find balance. For most people, it takes time. Ultimately, we try to find the true balance. To find that natural balance, unlock your true intent, your true dream of life. Cook with your life ingredients. Ask what is most important in your heart.

Process # 26: Discover three to five things that are sacred and important to the quality of your life. Plan to go with these. Identify and take action. Make sure that it is a tangible product. The reason I get up each morning and feel alive is? It is the force, the drive for every moment.

When someone gives you a cup of water, return the favor by digging a well. One reason why I recently returned to the mountain in Wu Dang was to establish a business that will help the town's people to set up a distribution channel. After two years, I walked away. It was to help build the temple, build a playground, to teach people how to do business and help them by teaching them skills of wealth. You live in your own vision. Be disciplined and trust in yourself. When you are convincing others, you become a slave to others. Find freedom of living with no guilt and no self-judgment. When you compromise your original nature, you compromise yourself and the quality of your life.

Ask yourself why you grieve. What do you hold down in your heart? What do you put out that prevents God's gift from reaching you? What is your true purpose? All the various psychological techniques are not necessary when you open your heart. Don't cast yourself as a victim who is being prevented to receive the gift. Don't try to understand why, stumbling around trying to understand the barrier rather than going straight to your heart. You come into this life naked and you will leave naked. Take a good look. As long as you have one last breath, it is never too late to confirm the true intent of your life. It is never too late to open up your true heart. Are you willing to be truthful? Identify the barrier that stops you. Identify why the more you see the more you judge. Does it really make you a better person to judge someone else as a lesser person? Look into your heart and identify it. Then it will all merge and disappear. There is no vulnerability to block. Let go of the fear, then no fear exists. The devil laughs as each event in life penetrates your barrier, causing you to build it stronger. You are the slave of the devil when you do this. You are a slave when you feel unhappy, not sexy and not rich. I went to the cave to rediscover who I am again, to acknowledge that I am alive and to gain the greatest appreciation for the simple life in rural China. You too must go to the cave to rediscover who you are.

How do you destroy the barrier and feel the master within? Did you misinterpret your childhood wish or your parent's wish? Did you underestimate your ability? Are you publically holding up the sky and secretly peeing in your pants? I also was taking my mission to such an extreme. My Master *Li* wanted me to be who I wanted to be. She never asked me to pee in my pants. I misinterpreted her wish so vigorously and into an extreme. How much have you put pressure upon yourself? What have you done to yourself? What are you capable of today? Be who you are today. Look at yourself. Don't force yourself to be somebody you are not. That is fake intent. Come out of the fantasy and go back to the source. Rediscover, or reinstate your dream. Reconfirm the purpose of your living. You are in heaven. Use dialectical thinking. When you reach to your feelings, be clear every day on what your purpose is. Nothing can stop you from smiling. Nothing can hurt you. Realize that even though you are devoted to the spiritual path, you will encounter hidden problems. They will show up. You cannot expect others to change. Feel joy rising from the *Dan Tian*. Reconnect with spirit and feel you true purpose. Always keep your eye on the apple. Say, "I am in my dream. I live in my dream. I live in my heaven. Therefore, I don't have to fear not being in heaven."

Chapter 33

Be a Lovely Dummy

A wise man often appears as a fool. I learned a lot from my master. Not to judge people is for the greater benefit of my own spirit. Not to disturb and distress my own physical and spiritual life. Withdrawing from the fame and honor gives the pleasure that only you know. Learning to be a dummy is much more challenging than to be intelligent. When you find that you are willing to be a dummy and then enjoy being a dummy, you become a wise man. Return to simplicity and hold onto your true intent for immortality.

Tao is a completely selfish Tao. You must accept yourself before you will be accepted. You must forgive yourself in order to be capable of forgiving others. Only one in ten thousand people try to be nobody! Those of you who have ears let them hear. Those of you who have eyes let them see. Aspire to decrease who you are. When *Tao* rises one inch the devil rises one hundred feet. It is very difficult for Tao to gain ground. Come with nothing and go with nothing.

"*Wu Wei Er Wu Bu Wei*" is to, "Do nothing and leave nothing undone." "*Wu Wei*," is doing nothing. "*Wu Bu Wei*," means, "nothing can't be done." We say, "*Nan De Hu Tu.*" It's difficult to be a dummy. It also means, "It's great to be a dummy." Everyone tries to be wise or to be smart, and everyone wants to be in control of life. They want to be smart, in control, wise and to be so intelligent. One painter in ancient China, *Zheng Ban Qiao*, during the *Qing* dynasty, was famous for painting bamboo and ascribing to strict personality, character and spirit. He would rather be straight than bend to life. He'd rather live with a straight spine than bend down for mercy, or beg to live. He said that he was so grateful to be a dummy and that phrase has now become words of wisdom for Chinese people for hundreds of years. He taught us that it is great to be a dummy, even if it is hard to be a dummy. Once you really understand what it is to be a dummy, you are a truly brilliant, intelligent and wise person. This idea is hard to be understood by western culture.

From what I understand, after coming to the west for so many years, people in the west want to be smart. They want to be in control; they want to be told they look good; they look smart and that they're wealthy and successful. But people think that when I say it's okay to be a dummy and that I want to be a dummy, that I undervalue myself and that this would provide no validation for them. The West is so much into competition, competing over who is better, who is wealthier and who is more eager. The competitive nature in this country has made a lot of people not willing to be "second class." Everybody wants to be the best, to be in the front of the line and to be number one. In Taoist teaching, we love to be number two, we love to stand behind because, in China, there is a saying, "The bird that sings the loudest always gets shot first. The pig that gets the fattest is always slaughtered first." The more you try to be number one, the more challenge and the more attention you get also, the more enemies you make and the more pressure you put on yourself. It's so much pressure that you can't even function anymore. I have an adult friend in the U. S., whose parents put so much pressure on him in his early life. He was always told that he had to be number one. He had to be the best. Under that pressure, he was so afraid that he couldn't even pick up the dishes, couldn't even pick up the fork and knife to eat. "What if it's not perfect," he would think? He couldn't even function in school because, "What if he couldn't be the best?" So he started telling himself, "It's better to do nothing," because then I'm safe.

In China, it's our nature to withdraw our sharpness, put brilliance behind and be humble. My nature was so different when in1992, I came to this country and I started teaching *Tai Chi* and *Qi* Gong. A friend asked me, "How are your skills on *Tai Chi*? How good are you at Kung Fu and *Qi Gong* healing?" My natural reply was to say, "I'm still learning." My friend replied, "You can't say that! Nobody will pay ten dollars per class to study with someone who is not good enough." It was a culture shock to learn that being humble in this country was to be stupid. Being humble, you can't find a job and you can't find people to learn from you. You can't find a friend, because you're not sharp enough, not competitive enough, can't give them enough motivation. In fact, people who are willing to be humble and who are willing to be a dummy just happen to be a side mirror for someone who is aggressive. In China, we try not to be aggressive. We are peaceful and in stillness. You are in motion and we are in stillness. We make a perfect pair, two pieces of the puzzle. Just because I'm not aggressive and in motion doesn't mean that I won't accomplish the result. In fact, the still and peaceful person achieves higher goals and better results in life.

Wise people remain in the white part of the Yin/Yang symbol, the *Yang* part. Seventy-five percent of the time wise people are: positive, success oriented, accomplish great achievement and are reserved for goals. They allow themselves twenty-five percent for negative things. "Good plus not good equals joy; one-hundred percent joy, one-hundred percent wisdom. We allow ourselves to have imperfect and perfect in life." Imperfect happens to be great leverage for perfect. Life should have one hundred percent achievement, one hundred percent success. But life is not perfect. If it is perfect, then it will turn out to be imperfect. If you strive for perfection, then you are like somebody who seeks to use a map for life. Perfect can never come from outside. Perfect has to come from inside. The judgment of perfection has to come from inside. If we allow for a life with imperfection, then we build up great leverage. It's not called an excuse, but in the end it is a great excuse to balance our emotions and balance our intelligence. The human intelligence can be very blind. If we look for perfection, we become very imperfect. For that reason, we allow ourselves to be imperfect and then we happen to be very perfect. Because we are willing to be imperfect, in fact we may achieve perfection. We become one hundred percent perfect. We use imperfect to make perfect happen. Only the most foolish and stupid people try to look for perfection.

By being nobody we are a totally extraordinary somebody! An extraordinary somebody is based upon an ordinary somebody. It comes from loving yourself for who you are today. An unhappy self doesn't have value. The heart has a soul and it is emptiness. You have to invite spirit to come in. "What I do for me, I do for the world." Self-worth is recognizing that my life is in my own hands! So, if you dream, why dream small? *Tao* gives the capacity to dream big. Do not limit the way you dream and how you dream. Spiritual wealth is recognizing that God, *Tao*, has an abundance of wealth. Ask yourself, "Am I the one to receive this wealth?"

Every person maintains his or her destiny, yet it is a unique journey. How you participate, come and go is a unique journey. Never judge, or interfere with another person's journey. You can be a facilitator and an example, but you can't be an enforcer for another person's journey. Each person has a unique journey to work out. You can only be a totally compassionate facilitator in their journey. When each person's journey finishes, he or she goes on to the next journey. Let go of people in your life so that you allow them to move on and also, so that you can move on. Let your loved ones finish their journey without the burden of you holding onto them.

There is a kissing your own brown nose concept: If you question your master's ability to move you along, then you are calling your master stupid. Saying that you are not good enough is also calling your master stupid. Believe in yourself. Pick out what you want to take from life and be happy with it. The dialectical choice is choosing what resonates for your spirit. Choose the perfect from the imperfect. Don't judge. Don't assume that the voice will come from the most spiritual person. Accept the principle and not the product.

Lao Tsu taught people to be like water. You constantly create new logic. Be aware of this and keep dropping this logic. The greatest people live with the greatest perceived loneliness. They have the greatest joy, but no one to share it with. Can you live it, can you just live without seeking confirmation from others? The greatest achievement is to live in spirit. Being spirit is to enjoy. Being human is to describe. "I know I'm a dummy. I know I'm pathetic. But I know my spirit is brilliant. So I put trust and faith in that."

Process #27: When you find yourself in judgment, when you find yourself in the negative, as soon as you catch it, think to the opposite side of your emotion.

Intelligence can fool you where wisdom can save you. Wisdom gives hope and determination to walk the path. Understand that the journey is walked alone. Practice unconditional love. Live and let live. You have the greatest expectation of your own expectations. When you don't live up to your own expectations, you punish yourself. By doing this, you commit chronic suicide. Allow your self to live and to let live also. Allow yourself to be different. Ask, "Do I give myself opportunity to be different? Do I allow and give myself new opportunities?" Change the tone of the word "hard" to, "it is quite a challenge." When you approach things as a challenge, as opposed to hard, you put yourself into a more joyful and excited energy. This brings the joy. Change to a "challenge."

Practice unconditional love with no value, or judgment attached to it. Unconditional love is not victimized if that love is not returned. God loves you! Say, "I love you," and mean it. I love you is different when you let the voice come from your heart with emotion. When you say it from the head, it is an intellectual love and is not heartfelt. Let the voice come from the spirit. It is merciful to see the pain in the devil's heart. Practice unconditional love. Your own self is the first one to practice with.

When you don't understand something, don't be afraid to ask. Only stupid people look for perfection. They think the world is designed to be one way, so all their life they look for perfection. Only when you acknowledge that the world is not perfect does it become perfect. If you are willing to honestly acknowledge that you are stupid, then you become intelligent. It is always easy to point a finger at others, but it takes great wisdom to point the finger at your own nose. Those who dare to point the finger at their own nose are the wisest people. *Meng Zi*, a Confucian disciple said, "Check yourself three times a day and you will become a wise man." Self-check three times a day. Point the finger to yourself. Why blame your parents for something that happened many years ago? Why be comfortable being pathetic? It's just an excuse to not grow. It is saying, "The outside world is too dangerous. At least I'm comfortable with how I feel." By doing so, you build a fantasy world.

Go beyond the concept of I and not I. Self and selflessness is equal to *Tao*. The greatest individual is the one who is servant to all. To conquer one's self is more challenging than to take down a city. Be willing to lie down for people's needs. Love has no need to attach, or detach. Love has no ego and no emotion to entertain. The lovely dummy is humble, she does not ask for an approving expression, or a return of appreciation. He will always do the same consistently. You don't have to live for appreciation of others, so don't ask or look for it. I serve *Tao*, not a letter of approval. When you serve humanity, serve each individual without ego or agenda, if not you become a slave to that agenda. Disengage from the game; ego only becomes a trap.

Your intent is to serve with purpose and passion, to be a healer. Be a spiritual person and enlighten people's drive. The reward is not worldly; it is a confirmation from *Tao*. In the virtue world it is a virtue exchange. Return to spirit is the motion of *Tao*. Adjust your original intent from that of wanting to be the greatest person others want, to one of serving yourself. Detach from the desire of getting, or losing. Serve from the bottom of your heart. A truly wise person must be a fool who lets energy pass by with no judgment to understand. With no agenda you can see the whole.

It takes a wise man to see a wise man. Live and let live. Respect others right to live. Live with integrity and without judgment, so that you can enjoy how others live. Let go of all your preconceived models. Be wise and compassionate. A heart for a heart and an eye for an eye concept only leaves the whole world blind. You live in your own heaven so why create an opponent? Men and women are different. Let go of models and respect other's needs. Men dominate the world with a sword and power. Women dominate the world through men. The woman is much more powerful.

Chapter 34

Get Out of Your Fantasy: Break the Illusion

Do you live for yourself, or do you live for others? For whatever reason, many people live in a fantasy world of denial and escape from the reality of who they really are. They build a house on the sand of illusion without a strong foundation. Don't live in the expectations of others. When you put on the mask in the morning, is it because you enjoy and love yourself so much? You do not need to please others. Find your self-worth in place of being a slave of others' expectations. It is never too late to change, or to take off the mask. Stop running and face reality with a smile.

Lu Dong Bin, one of the eight immortals, was on his way to take a public service test in front of the emperor. If he did well he'd be appointed to a political position, acquiring prestige and power for himself and his family. The group he traveled with stopped along the way to spend the night at an inn where *Lu Dong Bin* met a beggar who offered him a pillow to rest his head. During his sleep, *Lu* dreamed that he scored the highest of anyone on the imperial examination and he was appointed a government official position. After a series of promotions, *Bin* became prime minister. Bad luck then struck. He was framed and thrown into jail for crimes he did not commit. His family was ruined and lived a terribly poor life after that. Having experienced this dream, *Lu* awoke to find him-self lying on a golden beam with the beggar *Zhongli Quan* next to him. *Lu* recognized that the beggar was an immortal and so, he immediately abandoned his desire for public service to follow *Zhongli Quan* and study *Tao*.

Life is a dream! In one dream you can experience your whole life and come to realize the true meaning of life. Get out of your fantasy and break the illusion. In a story from ancient times, a scholar heard about people in the city of *Hang Dan*. He heard that they walked very elegantly and beautifully. He said, "I'm a scholar, I want to learn. I want to learn to walk like people in *Hang Dan*." So he traveled a long distance, finally reaching *Hang Dan* City. Once there, he followed behind people and copied how they walked, their leg movement, their arm movement, their expression. He studied them for a month. Despite how hard he tried, he couldn't learn the walk for the reason that he wasn't from *Hang Dan*. He tried so hard to copy them that he soon forgot how he walked naturally. A month later he couldn't walk at all. He had to crawl home. In his attempt to be someone who he wasn't, he lost himself. Each man is unique. There is no place like home. Don't try to copy the walk of *Hang Dan*.

Process #28: Paint a picture of what you want instead of the steel box that you have created. Show me that person. Keep this person in your heart and soul! Don't ever take your eye from it.

If you believe it, then God will deliver. Be consistent with what it is you want. When you come to the doorstep of heaven, do not say that you want three more chances. "I love my family! They are me and I am they. We are family." If you make your character come to life then you will win an Oscar. "I am my own favorite character." Don't look outside to identify and look for approval. Drop the ego!

We all hold onto emotions that we carry like insurance— something that we pull out as an excuse. Do you have one general excuse that you often use? Something to excuse your-self like, "I must take care of my children; somebody has to do the dishes; somebody has to go to work; I'm too busy; I'm tired; I was abused as a child; I had a horrifying first marriage." There is so much lack of self-confidence and you try to find a reason for it. Another thing we, as humans, do, is to fantasize. When we have a problem, we try to go to an opposite side and say that we don't. Do you know why some boys and some girls are so challenged to find a right partner? They can't seem to trust anyone, so they frequently change girlfriends and boyfriends.

Females compare and put down other females. Males put down others on intellectual strength. Females compare and judge sexiness, femininity, or perhaps success among stronger females. As a result people desire to stay young and sexy. Try to learn what it is that you often do, or how you often perform. From a philosophical standpoint, it is all very pathetic. You lose track of your life's true goal. Instead of focusing on your goal, you fight another person and lose track of why you live. The crane stands alone among all the roosters and chickens. This is a very visual way of looking at it. You are being a crane that compares itself to roosters and chickens. What a lousy and boring crane. The dragon is meant to fly in the sky. The warrior is meant to go to the battlefield. You don't want to compete over who's taller right under the table. The world is much bigger. There are more unknown and challenging things waiting out there. You are special. Go out and meet the challenges. Prove to yourself that you are special. It is only the rooster and chicken that you compare to. Go stand among the cranes if want to compare.

We always search out people who are not as good so that we can say, "I feel more valuable." Don't compare to those who are not your peers. When you are a dragon go to the big ocean, don't play in a little lake. Do you have the vision that you can have the whole ocean to swim in? Take your vision out of your house. Don't fight with your little circle or little community.

In the barren north, there is a dark sea, the Celestial Lake. There is a fish living there that is several thousand li in breadth and no one knows its length. Its name is *Kun*. There is also a bird called *Peng*. Its back is like Mount Tai and its wings are like clouds across the heavens. It spirals up to ninety thousand li, beyond the clouds and the wind. With blue sky above, it heads to the South Sea. A quail, by the marsh, laughs saying, "Where does he think he is going? I bob up and down a few feet, fluttering among the weeds and bushes. This is perfection in flying. What is he up to?" This is the difference between small and great![4]

Chuang Tsu is describing the *Yuan Shen,* or original spirit, and how powerful and free it is. Do not sidetrack yourself fighting in a little box. Don't play ping-pong under the table. You cannot get taller than the table, and your ability has been completely limited. Worse yet, you see yourself as very powerful because you see a little sky. It is like the frog at the bottom of the well. The bird and the frog have a dialog. "Hey Mr. Frog, how are you doing down there?" Don't limit the size of your vision and your ability to fly. Always understand that your intelligence and your vision have limitations. Know your own limitations! Never try to pretend that you are good at something that you're not good at. Some people so vigorously guard their weakness. The strong human is the one who is willing to admit weaknesses. Always be nice, compliment and be willing not to be the best at things you are weak with. On the flip side, don't give false compliments or you will lose that person's respect. Admit what you don't know and be humble. Once you lower yourself and lower your guard then the opportunity to learn is created. The door opens for learning. Do not be afraid to tell a joke about yourself. Do not be afraid to show your weakness. If the others

---

[4] *Chuang Tsu,* Inner Chapters, pg. 9.

laugh at you then they have bigger problems to clean up for themselves. If that happens, then you can walk away. Your weakness can also be your biggest strength. Allow it to create great strength. This is wisdom!

Taoism is about logic. I am here to teach you how to live without it! Drop the patterns! You have lived in logic for so many years that you now believe your logic. The human is such a fool! We cage ourselves. We give ourselves such a limited place to live. Look what happens with the simple question, "What is your name?" All identity comes with it, and you are trapped! When you learn to live without the "I" you will find the true "I." When you live without logic, you find logic. You can live in freedom when you drop the "I," when you drop the logic. This affects you physically, spiritually and emotionally. You corner yourself. Do the, "Dance On The Table" test. If you can backtrack on logic and go back to the original condition, and then change the logic, then you can dance on the table.

The sword is always a double-edged sword. We live in an illusion. See the truth! Some people see one side, while others see two sides. The truth is that there are three sides and even four sides. Conscience is equal to kindness. This is the original human nature. Taoism says that no logic is indeed logic. *Yin-Yang* is a black dragon and a white dragon that merge into a new black and white dragon, a healing dragon. Can you see something as both? Look with open mind and open heart. Not one or the other. Both can be true. There is always possibility. When they merge, you think it's complete but there is a hidden level, the middle. Learn to go beyond and above what you see and what you believe. I tell you that, "What you know is limited by the tools that you have to see with." The more tools you gain, the more you have to see. Reflection, your reaction and response, is based upon your own understanding, your emotion and your intellect. Does that make it true?

Be as real as you can in each moment. Live in reality. Don't live in fantasy. Let your feet be on the earth. Allow yourself to be in the dirt and mud. Accept it! Be with it! Why don't you allow this? It is all good, so be real! *Taoism* is very practical, so live it. Accept without denying so that you can go beyond. The first step is to accept. See the mud first, and then perhaps you can see it as honey. Don't bypass reality to get to wisdom. Wisdom comes from reality. First, be human and then you can be immortal. Be ordinary, and then you can become extraordinary.

God gives the gift of reality. Why do you avoid, fantasize and pretend? You only create more confusion. See the truth, deal with it, and then transcend. You are here to learn to live in no logic. First you need to stir up your understandings of logic. You need to get confused, and then you can clear it out. Learn the illogic of logic. Logic is illogical; it is based upon limited human understanding.

Feel the God-given gift. First feel grounding and feel yourself. Without this you have nothing to work with. Be real and acknowledge the feelings that you have. You need to be able to know this about yourself. You have been living in so much fantasy, denial and fear. Can you open your heart and spirit to invite the sunshine in? Through our growing up, our true spirit is often locked into the little cabinet under the sink. Originally, this was for many reasons. But now, we continue to keep it locked ourselves. We have been inside for so long that we get used to the darkness. We no longer know what the world is like outside. We don't open the door because, "What if?" Break out of the comfort zone under the sink. Although it is an illusion, it's also very real. Can you entertain your spirit towards your comfort zone and your discomfort zone? Life is in the movement and life is in the flow. Always check and challenge your comfort zone. Break your mold. Breaking from expectations is scary, but it is also so very freeing.

If nothing can penetrate to the true heart, if you are living too much intellectually, then you are fantasizing. Everything is an energy flow. If you constantly find yourself wanting to translate it, or to understand it, then you pollute your heart and you suffer from this. Giving your power to another person makes that person a persecutor. If the other person doesn't approve of you, you feel lousy and victimized. Make your decisions and don't care what others say. Make the right decision and follow through with it. Honor the principle at the moment you make your choice or decision. Also, mind your own business! Life is so simple. Don't make it complicated. Make sure that you are responsible for your own prosperity and spirituality.

Chapter 35

I Finally Learn How to Fly

I often ask the question, "What will the construction worker say when he falls from the roof of a high rise building?" He laughs and yells, "I finally have learned how to fly!" That is how we beat death, rather than let death haunt our spirit. When I was learning martial arts, there were eight people throwing knifes at me. I had to learn how to stay alive with a blindfold on. My master taught me how to stay alive even when there are ten thousand arrows shot at me at the same time. There is no concept of death. There is no arrow coming at you at any given time. Yield and live like water. It just it!

In 1994 I went on my first vacation, going to the island of Jamaica. We flew from Miami to Jamaica. During the middle of the flight, it was lunchtime, and while everyone was eating, we encountered severe turbulence. Dishes flew in the air, and the plane rocked violently as if it was going to fall from the air. Passengers screamed and cried as if the end of their life were here. I sat next to an older lady who was probably eighty some years old. She quivered, her face was pale and she shook. She started to cry. At that moment, I secured myself and then reached to her. I said to her, "Isn't this cool that we are like a bird flying in the air?" Then we laughed, we followed the plane pattern and I would say, "Left turn, okay, right turn, okay, up, down..." and I was able to entertain her and take her attention away by telling her that a plane can be like a bird flying. Be one with the plane and feel the motion of the plane, rather than be afraid. At just that moment the plane went back to normal and everybody was back to normal and of course very emotional. For the rest of the trip, I told the following story to this older woman.

There was a time in China when I was in martial arts training and we came to a cliff on the mountain. My martial arts teacher, Master *Guo*, was testing me and told me to jump off the cliff. I listened to my master and thought, "Okay, my master told me to jump off." For three seconds I thought, "Is that real? He wants me to jump off?" And then, the next second, I said, "Okay Master, let me jump." So I walked forward and was ready to jump. My master smiled, grabbed my shirttail and brought me back saying, "Good, you just passed the test to beat death." Master *Guo* said, "As a martial artist, the biggest fear is death, and in martial arts situations, fear of death always occurs." He said,

"You came to the edge, you didn't see death, but listened to me. Not only listened to me, but had the courage to put it into action. This means you have already beaten the concept of death."

If I feared death, I would be busy experiencing the fear and trying to find a way to defeat death. I would try to find all the possibilities so as not to die, using all the techniques I know not to die. Master *Guo* taught me, when people fall off a cliff, they have two choices. They can choose to laugh and say, "I finally learned how to fly," or they can choose to scream, pounding to the bottom of the valley and dying. He said there are two ways to choose death: the first way you never die. If you say and sing, "I finally learned how to fly," your spirit will already have left your body to the enlightenment before the physical body pounds to the death. The second way is to scream. The spirit is also going to leave, but it will leave at the moment the body pounds into the bottom of the valley. Then we experience the horror and pain of the fall, and then, the spirit will bring that fear to the next journey of the life. The same way of dying can either bring joy to the next journey or it can bring fear and suffering. That choice is strictly yours.

I am not saying that everyone can consciously make this choice when facing death's challenge. Not everybody can say, "Okay, I can fly like a bird." But what it really means is that every single day we need to go beyond that fear of living and the fear of dying. Stress and difficulty in life can make you afraid of living. When it comes to situations of illness, terminal illness or an accidental tragedy that brings you face to face with death, these can also make you afraid to live. We face the fear of living and the fear of dying. Every day we need to go beyond this fear to live joyfully and have the right attitude toward each day; the right, good attitude of living with joy. Live in the moment. Then, when the death moment does occur, you are able to automatically feel like a bird flying in the air. Then there is no death.

You are in the heaven already! You are not waiting to go to heaven; rather you are growing into heaven. If you are waiting to get picked up, you will be waiting forever. You will never get picked up! Your belief about heaven can be your trap. When you are dancing with the devil, use caution not to become the devil. Can you see yourself without a mirror? There's a beautiful world to explore. Take advantage of it. Is it patient doctor or doctor patient? Refocus your drive and determination. It's not a failure of your past beliefs. Rather, it is a redirection of your thought system. If you love your child to the ultimate, then be willing to let go of that child. Love is to leave your child to itself to grow. Love *Tao*. Be an extraordinary human. The dragon can't be seen, and yet, it can be seen. *Tao* can't be described. I can only paint my own dragon. Use these principles to discover your own principles. Walk in the battlefield with confidence and retreat from the battlefield with pride.

Chapter 36

Life is Not a Disaster
Crisis is an Opportunity

Life is just a journey, a moment and an opportunity. In Taoist belief, "My life is in my own hands, not in heaven's." The purpose of coming to this planet for a moment is to enjoy life, to build credit and to create happiness. To ride this opportunity, practice virtue and return to stillness by cultivating internal alchemy, leading you to your final departure from the material world. Engage life by actively practicing *Tao*, cultivating virtue and entertaining life.

Some preachers scare people and force them into religion, to buy a ticket to heaven. This makes for a passive life. Life is not a disaster. There is not only one pass or gateway to heaven. You will not go to heaven because of fear. We are all growing into heaven. We are not going to heaven. Taoist philosophy emphasizes practicing a perfect physical life (*Ming*), merged with cultivating essential nature (*Xing*). Combining these two ingredients together makes for immortality. Otherwise, you will have to return to this material life's journey time after time until you "get" it. Taoism brings information to tell people that, "You can control your own reincarnation."

Wei Ji means that crisis is opportunity. A crisis presents an opportunity. However, you have to empty yourself first in order to get the fresh opportunity. Even death can provide opportunity. Death of the old self allows for opportunity of a new self. So enjoy the ride and ask yourself what opportunity you want to bring to the new journey. Mindful intelligence can fool you, whereas, wisdom will save you. In every moment, you affect the people around you. Be bold! Give the people around you a new journey. Do not be under a wrong assumption of death. Be the man so that you can be God. If you are a diamond, you are always a diamond. A diamond in the mud is still a diamond. Come to the realization that, "I am perfect as myself." You are perfect in your imperfection." I am too sexy for my clothes," so to speak.

Start a new chapter in your life. Do it now, and do it well! There is no value in getting stuck. There is no value in saying, "If only I had this, then I could succeed." What you don't have, create. The old hard drive, the old way of thinking provides no value to you any longer. So just reformat it! You never know what event will have great value in the future. Always choose good over bad. Always choose the best memory to share with the self, the world and others. Turn an event into a catalyst for good results. Turn events into experience and wisdom, rather than suffering and pain.

Can you see the success when you feel the disasters? Of course! Opportunities always arise from crisis. When you set yourself up for failure, you will fail. In Taoist practice, we dislike for people to make excuses all the time. When you label yourself, you create a limit; you put yourself into a certain show. Then, you use this as an excuse all your life for not doing new things. This only hurts you. This corners your self. It boxes you into a certain category. Know that you can only describe this moment. You cannot know what the next moment will bring. Let me teach you. You can do this. You are your own creation. I teach you all how to think differently.

When a crisis comes, we can run for cover or we can see the other side of the coin, and then turn it into opportunity. At four years old, I had a little argument with my cousin next door. His father and my father are brothers and my cousin is one year older than I. My uncle came back from Hong Kong. They had the privilege of going to Hong Kong and so were relatively rich. He came back from Hong Kong and the first toy, I remember, was one that he brought back, a truck, a children's toy. My family was the poorest in the whole village. At four years old, I saw this truck, the first toy that I ever saw in my whole life. I sat down and just tried to play with this boy, this cousin. He pushed me and said, "You can't play. This is not yours, and get out." He said, "How can you play with us."

So probably my emotions and ego were aroused and I pushed him back. I smashed the truck. This all created big trouble. His mother and father jumped up to punish me. They demanded that my parents pay for the truck. That toy was pretty costly at that time in China, and there was no way that my parents could afford to pay for it. My father had just come home from hard work. He heard about this and didn't want to hear any explanations from me. He picked something up and whacked me with it. He hit me until there were bruises. It was on the night before New Year's—New Year's Eve. New Year in China is a very important day. I felt so bad that he wouldn't even listen to me or defend me—nothing—so I ran away to the mountain behind our house. I hid behind a huge rock all night. Below, I heard the village people celebrating and shooting off firecrackers. My parents were looking for me and I wanted to come out, but also I just wanted to be alone. I sat there in the moment, soaking pain, when suddenly a voice came to me and said, "Wow! There are millions of children sitting in pain, just like me, all over the world." At that moment, I said, "When I have money some day, I will buy trucks for all of them." It was a moment of joy for me to turn this all around. From one second to another I turned my emotions around. I went back home and pretended nothing had happened.

Chapter 37

You Can't Change the World, but You Can Change Yourself

Many people want to change the world with physical force or emotion. There are very few people willing to change themselves to change the world. The world never functions through your own will. You either become prostitutes (slaves) of the material world or you become masters. You don't live for others but live for yourself. The quality of your *Yuan Shen* or original spirit sets the measurement for how you see the world. A stronger *Yuan Shen* gets you to enjoy the world more than the ordinary person. The material world only disturbs the stillness of your *Yuan Shen*. We can learn to stay in stillness to face uncertainty. We can learn not to take any disturbance from the outside world. Although a pebble may ripple the surface of the water, know that the pond is unfathomably deep. Calm your mind and intent, balance and harmonize the *Xing* and *Ming*. Stay focused on the purpose of your life. Detach from the need of the self. Accept and be loyal to the true self, and then, you will change the world around you forever.

Everybody maintains a destiny of their own, yet it is a unique journey. How they participate, come and go, is a unique journey. Never judge or interfere with another person's journey. You can be a facilitator and an example, but you can't be an enforcer for another person's journey. People have their own unique journey to decipher for themselves. You can only be a one hundred percent compassionate facilitator in their journey. Turning the wheel from "myself" into how "I" can be the best facilitator for their unique journey. When our journeys finish we go on to the next journey. Learn to let go of people in your life so that you allow them to move on, and also, so that you can move on. Let your loved ones finish their journey without the burden of you holding onto them. The world does not dance for you. It has its own rhythm. Can you change the world one iota with your will? No! You can only impact on it. If you can change your world, then the world changes. You must begin with the self. The world will always follow its own way. Change yourself and the world changes.

Find the master within. Don't assume that you are enlightened to master others! Be the master of your own. Be a personal guide through example but not a teacher. Walk the talk. Ask yourself how you can help. To introduce the tasty apple to others, you have to first taste it yourself. I can do it. I am the master of my own. Never limit your potential. Dream Big! Don't limit the creativity of your dream. Continue to be your dream. Be the dream-weaver of *Tao*. When the lion king is absent from the forest, then the monkey becomes the master. The true master makes masters. You can be a master of your own. You can't run away from your own devil by trying to master others.

Couples tend to look alike when he is in her and she is in him. *Tao* is equal to the *Yin* and the *Yang*, not just one or the other. Two people can be completely different, but they must have each other in soul and heart for a good relationship. There are both the white eye and the black eye in the *Yin Yang* symbol. Companionship doesn't ask for anything. Live and let live! Do you have the wisdom to allow your partner to be him or herself? Have the mercy to forgive. Why force what is different to be the same? Do you have the wisdom to allow your partner to be different than what you are?

The sword of wisdom is always hanging over your head. You can try to run, but you can't run from your own sword. People can never run from their own conscience. You must clean the mud from the water once and for all. Life is a triangle game! Master the game and play a great game. Play a good damn game! Trust yourself the way you expect others to trust you.

Show in actions that you are healthy, motivated and enthusiastic. Conquer your own world and allow others to conquer their own world.

The three top things to possess when you act are: love, compassion and understanding. Knowing when enough is enough often leads to great happiness. "*Zhi Zu Chang Le*" means, "Knowing enough, often happy!" Believe that humankind is healthy and that they don't need you to heal them. You must let go of the bottle's nipple. Every phrase is full of Taoist wisdom.

"Those who know don't talk. Those who talk don't know. Keep your mouth closed. Simplify your problems. Mask your brightness. He who has achieved this state is unconcerned with friends and enemies."[5]

Follow my footsteps. Walk the talk. Tell yourself, "I am pure and very clear in my life purpose. May I be a model to you!" Find your weakness and fix it. Don't pretend to not see it and not fix it. Take care of it. When the weakness becomes a crisis, then you will cry. The wise man sees all dimensions. When you know your own weakness, why do you just sit there? You have all these needles in your butt! This is not comfortable, yet you keep sitting there! You just hope that you'll bleed less tomorrow. This is pathetic! I hope those sitting on the needle make the choice to change their chair. At least know how to wiggle your butt!

---

[5] Tao Te Ching, Lao Tsu, translated by Gia-Fu Feng and Jane English, pg 58 (Chapter 56)

To fix family, you must go in with complete compassion and love. Bringing harmony will bring life to the whole family. Do not bring bad feelings to the family. Be the one to make the grand finale! You are not there to break it up. Be there to celebrate! Fix yourself, and then, there is nothing to fix in your family. Keep your eye on the gem, the ultimate purpose. In the end you have only yourself and your family who will bear with you. When you have problems with your family, you will have problems in the world. Bring harmony to your family to bring harmony to your purpose.

Bring courage and love. Once you fix yourself, the world is beautiful.

Chapter 38

Take Action

There was a general in ancient times, he often talked about military strategy on paper and thought that he was the greatest general. But when he came to the battlefield, he was easily defeated. Many daydreaming people talk and talk, but they never put their intents into practice. When you don't take action, you do not have a harvest. People often fear taking action because of the unknown. They are fearful to take action lest the sky will fall. Their life gets stuck without joy. My master taught me that the dish you cook yourself always tastes better and is more fragrant than the dish someone else cooks for you. Stand up to participate and take action. Participate in life bravely and joyfully. Then, whatever the harvest, it will bring you joy and satisfaction.

Experience comes from mistakes. Failure is the mother of success.

It is not a shame what the few evil people do in this world. Instead, it is what the many good people do not do that is the real shame. When a bird poops on your head, move. When crap happens, take action. If you stay there and try to clean it, you get crapped on again! Do something as soon as possible so you don't get stuck. A man who lives without a goal is like a walking dead man. Exercise yourself and exercise your spirit. Exercise your goal and stop walking like a dead man. Stop running like a chicken without a head. That is really pathetic.

Get up every day with a smile and take the action that you believe in. Use the three "D's:" devotion, dedication and discipline. Live in your own heaven and maintain the integrity of your heaven. Can you take action consistently every day, with joy and happiness? When you complain about life, life becomes harder. Don't persuade yourself out of participating. You are your own producer of your own show. This is a one-person reality show. Once the show is lost, don't lose the freedom! Enjoy the moment for the rest of your life. That is True Stillness.

If you get only eight of ten goals done in a day, then you must move the two undone goals to the top of the list for the next day. Work bottom to top and top to bottom. Happiness is selflessness. Start with a base happiness to construct an ultimate happiness. Setting and completing goals must become habit, but not an obsession. Have a general schedule for your day. Have a weekly and monthly to do list. You must work your family life into your to do list as well. Keep moving your butt. Start from where you are today, as that is the only place where you can start.

Have a passion for life, inclusive of everybody. Set goals for your material life function and for your spiritual life function. Every day construct a to-do list. Build a structure, but be flexible. Take action and in that action, feel and enjoy the stillness.

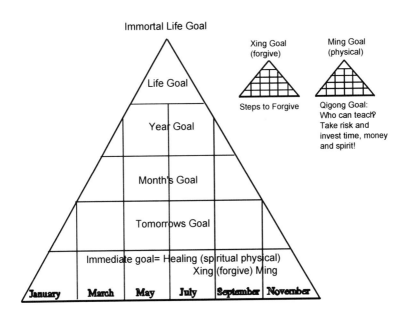

Level one of the goal triangle is the blueprint of your goal: know what is; who is capable of helping you; gather the necessary materials; make the choice of what to do with whom; build it and market it. You can't keep taking to achieve your goal. You must also give. Have passion for life, inclusive of everybody. Set goals for material life function and passion for life function. Every day, construct a "to-do-list." Keep lists and when you review the lists you may yet get enlightenment for your own *Tao*. If the immediate goal is to heal the spiritual or the physical, then set the steps to get there. Who can help, how to do it, and more!

Process #29: For the end of the book prepare a master plan for your life!

Mark the way to look for your sword. What you believe may not be real! If you believe the sword is here, then go and get it. The results, however, might not be what you expect. The sword may not be where you expect it to be. Be willing to take action. Don't delay action, rather solve it right there, so that you do not have to repeat your actions. Don't be afraid to leave your comfort zone. Don't delay, hoping that things will go away all by themselves. Delay is a form of self-abuse. Emotion can be a very powerful motivator if used in the right way.

Approach things with the Taoist concept, "I like it, when can I have it?" A clear self is a confident self. It is a healthy gain. You do not need the Mercedes, but recognize that you are capable of it. It is necessary to take action to flip the hamburger. Make flipping that hamburger the best time of your life. If you hate what you are doing, either stop doing it or do it better. Devote one hundred percent of your spirit and effort! Be your true self. Be your organic spirit.

Shop for organic clothing, drink organic tea, and think organic—www.OrganicSpirit.com! Refuse to think that you are old! Shake your butt in front of the mirror each morning. Think, "I am sexy. I am who I choose to be!" Be careful though. The thought, "I am," can put you into a box. Get out of your box to be a different person. If you continue to place yourself in a box, then you limit your thoughts, you limit your possibilities and you limit your choices. You don't need to be what you think you need to be. Rather, you can be whoever you want to be at this given moment. Be who you are, be what your heart and spirit tell you to be.

This is not only dreaming though. You must take action to be who you want to be. You must walk the talk! If you are forcing yourself, then you are not living *Tao*. Living must be spontaneous. My head may fly, but my spirit will stay grounded. You can chop my head, but my spirit will stay.   Never compromise your spirit!

In ancient times there was a man who, every day, was afraid to walk out of his house. His family and friends would ask him, "Why are you afraid to walk out of your house?"   He answered, "If I walk out of the house the sky will fall." The man was worried that the sky would fall, "*Ji Ren You Tian.*"   How many people live their life as though they have to hold up the sky? Are you afraid the sky will fall? Walk out of your house. Do not be unnatural! People are afraid to take action for fear of failure. They are afraid to fly. It is your time! It will be your time. Go live in it. Only then will you never have to worry. A lack of love and self worth cause you to worry that the sky will fall. It is only when you accept dying, that you can live! The phoenix rises from the ashes. Practice dying so that you can live! Have fun. Be the fool. Don't take everything so seriously. Don't "try" to live, just live!

Process #30: Process of Century: Get clear on your vision and goals. Get clear on emotional goals, spiritual goals, family goals and "now" goals. There are different levels of now goals.

Learn to set personal goals: An immediate goal is a now goal, dealing with what is in the moment. A future goal is tomorrow's goal. An ultimate goal is a long-term goal. In immediate goals, live moment to moment. React from the bottom of your heart and not from your head. You are acting from the moment in front of you, or the moment at hand. Find harmony, not denial and fantasy. Deal with logic and less illogic. If you are worried about sending a spider to heaven, do it if the spider is in your domain. The logical thing is to kill the spider so that it doesn't come to bite you in your sleep. The illogical, emotional side tells you to not kill that poor spider. Work with your natural instincts and not your emotional thoughts. If you are afraid of something, then deal with it. Don't let emotions ruin your life. Logically choose! Don't allow emotions to allow you to make illogical choices. Act and focus; do one thing and do it well.

When setting a goal, ask what the project is. Is it a logical or illogical goal, physical or emotional, achievable or fantasy? If it is achievable, do you have the money to do it? Will the family allow it? If the answer is no to either of these questions, then it is illogical. What outcome do I want should be the priority. Your spirit can advance time and space to allow it. If you set a goal, then you have to know that it is absolutely what you want. Logic and illogic often confuse the true logic: black dragon, white dragon, then true dragon; *Yin, Yang,* then true logic. Do you want to become immortal? Then don't ask whether it is logical or illogical. Rather, ask, "Am I the one?" When you are ready, the teacher will arrive. Stick with the true intent. Truly follow that goal, live in it and taste it! Identify the goal and believe that, "I am the one to achieve it." Goals are not achieved, in part, because you are not putting one hundred percent into them.

Set the timing to achieve a goal. "Next year," is too general. Next year is only an excuse to procrastinate. If you are making excuses, then God will travel to the next house to someone who actually wants to accomplish their goal in a specified time and manner. When you are ready *Tao* will come. By setting a time-line, you are registering yourself in God's schedule book. For example, by next year near, June 30, I will achieve my goal, is a definitive timeline. You state that, by this time or date, I want this to be done. If it is a logical timeline, then already, see yourself in the ranch home. Having done this for your-self, God delivers the ticket and reward. Be logical and illogical. Take action. Just because you set a timeline does not automatically mean that it will magically happen. You have to ask yourself what actions need to be taken. Your mental capacity has to totally be into it. If your mind is set to take advantage of God, thinking, "God will do it," then it won't happen. Be flexible like a dragon. Be willing to face fear. Use all the ingredients that God has given you. Your frame of mind can change everything, so exercise your options and choices.

In the third century A. D., China was divided by three powers, *Wei, Shu* and *Wu*. Each, respectively, controlled North, Southwest, and South China. One year, the state of *Wei* set off to attack *Wu*, and soon they arrived at the northern bank of the *Yangtze* River. *Wu*'s army was stationed at the other bank. *Wu*'s commander-in-chief, *Zhou Yu,* decided he could fend off the *Wei* army with arrows, but he'd need some one hundred thousand arrows. His problem was; how could he make enough arrows in such a short period of time? Just then, *Zhuge Liang,* Prime Minister of the state of *Shu* came for a visit. He said lightly that he could get the arrows in three days. He even signed a pledge, making himself liable for punishment should he fail to complete the task. He knew he couldn't manufacture that many arrows in only three days. So instead, he had the men use straw to make many boats and straw men. After placing the straw men on the boats they waited. As time went by the soldiers became restless. On the third night, however, winds from the east began blowing and so, *Zhuge Liang* invited *Lu Su* for a boat ride. The straw boats were tied together with strong ropes. *Zhuge's* fleet sailed toward the camp of *Cao Cao.* A thick mist had spread over the surface of the river. People could hardly see each other on the river. It was still dark when *Zhuge's* fleet arrived close to the *Cao* camp, *Zhuge Liang* ordered his soldiers to shout and beat drums to fake an attack. *Zhuge* and *Lu Su* simply sat inside one of the boats and drank wine, enjoying themselves. When the *Cao* camp heard the shouting and drum beating, they took it as a surprise attack by the *Zhou Yu* camp. They could not see anybody on the river, so they gathered ten thousand bowmen and ordered them to shoot arrows towards where the shouting and drum beating came. The straw boats and men were quickly shot full of arrows. After a while, *Zhuge Liang* ordered his fleet turn about to expose the other side of the boats. As this side was shot full of arrows, day broke and *Zhuge Liang* ordered his soldiers to return to their port. Upon returning to their camp, they collected more than one hundred thousand arrows from the straw.

Take action! Ask the question, "What am I willing to give and not willing to give? What can I do in this project?" If I don't have what I need, can I make straw boats to collect the arrows? Learn how to improvise. Do what you have to do to achieve your goal. Let go of your emotions and let go of your ego.

Identify your source and ability to accomplish your goal and then, make it happen. Walk the talk. Collect all the ingredients. If you are willing, then God will listen. Have the spiritual wealth. Your master is your Taoist spiritual business consultant. Are you hungry enough and willing to do the job? Do something extraordinary. Get out of your box. Invent your own straw boats to gather your arrows.

Ask what your immediate goal is and identify the source of health. Be flexible with your goal and ask if it is a logical goal or an illogical goal. For example, you may want to share your passion to meet and to help people. You must have a consistent passion for life and for everyone you meet. If you don't have joy in your heart, you will likely fail. You always have something that someone needs. Take advantage of that. Have passion for life. Joy is contagious. If you have joy, the devil will bow and step aside. Fear will allow the devil in and lead to death. Your heart and intent must be in the same place. Goals can change; so don't be rigid. Don't, however, change your immortality goal! Live well so that you can achieve your goal.

When I came to the United States, learning the language was my first step. I learned while working at McDonald's and by watching CNN. I had no car so I rode a bike, even in the snow.

I used my five senses to learn English. Initially, I also did not have a roof over my head, so I made friends and met a person who wanted to learn *Tai Chi*. In exchange for a room, I taught *Tai Chi* and paid one hundred dollars per month. At this point my heart sang. I had a job, a house to live in and I was making money. For my job, I learned how to fix the equipment and how to stock inventory. Soon I was offered a promotion to be sent to Beijing for a manager's position. The McDonald's in Beijing could house many, many people. I decided to decline that offer as I had other, more pressing goals. This is an example of staying true to your goals and not following distraction that are offered to you. By then I knew many people, had a driver's license and a VW Rabbit. People paid me forty-five dollars per hour to teach *Tai Chi* and to do healing work. After only three years in the United States I paid off a thirty thousand dollar debt to the people whom had brought me over from China. Do what it takes for your life. The spirit should never die. God always delivers what you need. If you trust God then don't bend to fear. Manifest your goals by following the blueprint. Have a consistent focus! As you move up the triangle carry your goal in your heart. Don't forget to use a triangle when setting your goal.

You must develop a goal and a vision for your life. If you have a vision, then stick with it. Surround it, hug it and make it become reality. Clean the mud from your diamond heart. Every person maintains a vision for his, or her, life. Be a sterling example for others. You are the owner of your vision. You must include everyone around you into your vision. Family life can be a vision. Determine the material and spiritual visions for yourself. A vision requires two processes to be realized. First, believe your vision and then, see you vision so that it becomes real.

First, choose the one apple to make you still. Once you choose that apple, then, you will have ten thousand choices available to you. All your other goals are for your family. When you have a goal, although you are committed to it, show non-attachment. Have a goal that will make you alive, find that goal and stick with it. Be sure to set the right goal. Externally, things may appear rough but internally, you are still. In the ocean ten thousand waves come from stillness.

Follow your nature, as *Tao* follows what is nature. Find a vision and a purpose. Go with what you are capable of. First, ride a white dragon that you are capable of riding before jumping onto a dragon that is too big. What you ask for, *Tao* delivers. Stillness is a metaphor. Unless you know action, there can be no stillness. Go from "*Wu* Ji to *Tai Ji* and *Tai Ji* to *Wu* Ji,"—stillness to motion and motion to stillness. Set immediate goals! If you can't conquer your immediate goals, how can you expect to conquer the ultimate goal of immortality? You must crawl before you walk. You must walk before you run. All emotions are one and the same!

Elixir of non-doing is formed in the void sky.

The dust speaking out shows emotions of human kind.

We sing the song of tranquility on the way to the immortal road.

Dancing the *Tai Chi* in the palace of *Dao*.

How many fools not awaken himself?

That immortal elixir is formed inside your tummy.

Arms pulling sun and moon together east, west, north and south.

Golden elixir formed in *She Li* that is unable not to tour in the ultimate mystery world. [6]

Process # 31: Imagine yourself ten years from now and share it in the present tense. Also, imagine yourself in fifty years.

When dreaming, why dream small? You don't know your potential, so why place limits? When you become clear on your vision you know what is needed to get there. When you are this clear, and your life has a purpose; when the direction, motivation and architecture are already set, then all you will need to do are the accessory jobs. Make it more beautiful and then it's done. When it comes to goal setting, our logic is often is based upon what we have experienced. Your intelligence and your ability are limited, so you tie your own hands and feet. However, when you speak dialectically you have total freedom and you can be clear about what you truly want.

When you live as if the future is now, you can take the actions to position yourself into that space and make it happen. See yourself clearly, so that you can know what's needed to get to where you want to be. You must get clear about what's top on your goals triangle. Then, a plan of action can be taken. It's like a pyramid, the gem is at the top, but the foundation must be very

---

[6] Conference Hall, Yun Xiang Tseng

strong. Proper action must be taken to meet your goal, or it remains a fantasy.

Process # 32: Have ready by the end of the book a very crystal clear blueprint for five and ten years from now.

The blueprint helps you to understand the necessary and practical steps. This is how you get to your master within. We have all been collecting for many years. We all have a giant, "Master Within." We just need to unlock the door. Allow the giant dragon to be awoken. If not, it just falls asleep in you. We all have the motivation. Seize your goal and take the actions necessary to keep the dragon awake. Attach and then detach. See and not see. The eye of my spirit never comes off the gem. The human part of me just keeps walking and taking action. The goal setting is not ambition, yet it is ambition. Do it with joy, with fun and with purpose to entertain the spirit. If you attach to the concepts of losing or gaining, or power and self-worthiness, then you will have troubles. Be a free spirit. You create limitations when you attach to the feeling of it.

Most people live day-by-day, living in the moment like a hippie. "If," sets a condition for failure. Then, you will never be; you are not; and it is only a possibility. By negotiating "if" with God, you put yourself in a category to dance with the devil. Negotiating makes you a slave and it means you are not being your own self. Saying, "If I only had money!" How pathetic is that? My Master *Guo*, while I stood on a Dragon Head, dangling three hundred feet above ground said, "I rather you fall and shame me here, than go into the community and shame me."

Dedication, devotion and discipline towards your passion will bring the motivation that gets you up every morning. Make it a very realistic goal. What do cherish every day that makes, or creates your entire world? What matters to you most? What feeds your soul and spirit? What is most important to you? What is the nutrition and food for your mind, body and spirit? Fear can be conquered, or it can be multiplied. Choose which side of the fence you wish to be on. When you choose to allow God or *Tao* abide within, then, you forever exempt from the devil.

Chapter 39

Healing Without Medicine

In the past thirty years, I have showed countless people the Taoist method for healing themselves without medicines. Illness is a symptom of imbalance. The illness is not a crisis. All you have to do is to find your way back to balance. Instead of searching for doctors and medicines, learn to return to stillness and identify the root of your imbalance. The exercises of *Tai Chi*, *Qi Gong*, and meditation help people to discover a way of self-healing from the internal, regardless of whether it is emotional, physical or spiritual. These are techniques to prevent disease, or to return from disease to a healthy balance.

You can heal your body through a simple self-scanning technique. For this to work, you must patiently and faithfully scan every day. You scan with stillness. Do this scan eighteen times, from head to foot.

Lay down on your back, with arms spread at your sides and hands cupped with palms faced down. Feel as if you are floating on water. The head and body must connect. Let this principle sink in, "Every day I am the leader on my life stage, but there are ten thousand people watching me with a radar. Everybody is going to judge me as either good or bad. I just accept that! I have no attachment so that I can see myself clearly, without fantasy. I must see myself clearly so that I can minimize my tail, making it more difficult to be caught." Slowly scan your body from the top of your head, to the soles of your feet. Scan your body, doing nothing and leaving nothing undone. Relax, breathing normally into the lower belly—the *dan tian*. To maximize the power of scanning, you must scan your organs with total compassion. Scan with love and patience.

After doing the head to foot scan eighteen times, you next place your hands, with palms down where the ovaries would be if you were, or are, female. The hands have a pulsating, dispersal energy, that reverses aging. Work your hands on the reproductive organs, the kidneys and the *dan tian*. Enjoy the moment and be patient for every pulsation. Silently observe the radiating, pulsating energy and no matter what it is, "It just it." Don't attach to it and feel it.

Next, a third step is optional and works with a known disease that you might have. Deal with the disease as if it is illogical. Move your hands to the area of the disease. For males the left hand is beneath the right, and for females just the opposite. Patiently, show love and patience to the area of disease. Show unconditional mercy and love. Pay attention to the disease and visualize ten thousand arrows of molecules radiating into the area. Breathe in, and breathe out, allowing the dust to be removed from your mouth on the out breath. After this, place both palms over the *dan tian*. Envision an image spiraling downwards from the touch, depositing *Qi* into the *dan tian*. Perform this for three to four minutes while lying down. Do these scans with patience, mercy and love. Once again, no matter what it is, "It just it." Don't dwell on either good or bad. Finally, seal the *dan tian* by massaging it circular with the palms, three to six circles clockwise and three to six circles counter clockwise. Dry wash your face with your hands. Dry wash the neck, shoulders, body and etcetera. Don't forget the concept, "I am my own patient. I am the master within. I have passion for life." This exercise is used to stir up stinky, or stale, *Qi*—vapor energy.

Mysticism incorporates unconventional thinking. Advanced thinking is what we call our spiritual reality. It is indeed spirit reality. It is not *Shi Shen* (intelligence) reality or human reality. We are encouraging people to explore their spiritual reality, and to discover a new paradise, rather than be forced into a paradise that is defined by mere human intelligence. Masters can only bring the student to the door. All students follow their own path to that door. Spirituality has already formed before you read this book. Today, I only teach this

Taoist paradise to you. It is like a Caribbean paradise. I can only describe one concept of my Taoist heaven for you. It is based upon my Taoist logic. I describe your Master's concept. It is you who, based upon this description, will create your own perception. Everyone learns the skill to put their perception and my perception together, to create an ultimate paradise for their own spirit. You find the opportunity to reconstruct your perception and eventually return home. There is no absolute method, or description. The more I describe the more I screw you up. I can only describe the feeling and taste of it. I hope that you are able to create an image of it, and to also taste and feel it for yourself. In the end, however, you are the one who must create the image. I am *Yin* and you are *Yang*. Together we can merge to find the hidden dragon.

Humans are mystical animals. This mysticism can screw us up and it can make us wonderful. It is for you to learn about your illogical intelligence. We get so sidetracked into a particular reality that what we know, is all we will allow ourselves to know. Be brave and allow another reality to exist. Allow the possibility. Allow the fifty percent opportunity. Our brain function is very interesting. Brain wave! Our thinking patterns can be changed, a lot. The pattern of thought that you vibrate can project a different brain wave. Invite the spirit with you. Why is the spirit often not loyal to a body? When you extend an invitation, then, you encourage the spirit to want to stay. You want your spirit to fall in love with your body.

Mysticism leads you to unconventional thinking. It is what we call our spiritual reality. But don't deny that you have a human reality at the same time. We are explorers. It's exciting to discover a new paradise! You are being shown how to construct your own paradise. The master brings the student to the door. The student must walk through the door, on their own path, to create their own reality

Chapter 40

Listen to Your Intuition

Life often entertains people with material and emotional concern. The intelligent spirit, or *Shi Shen*, often guides people to defend, or to be, offensive in their life. Their spirit remains in unrest day after day. Original spirit, *Yuan Shen*, however, can guide you toward the right path, despite your struggle with *Shi Shen* or intelligent spirit. Your conscience guides you to do the right thing, to take the right path. Listen to your own intuitive, guidance. Do not let emotions distract your conscience. If you faithfully exercise you body and mind, you will gain the ability to avoid any disaster in life. Enriching your spirit allows you to gain opportunity for immortality.

It is easy to lean to God for a decision; however, you must learn to make your decisions on your own. Flow with the dragon and don't fight it. When you take feeling, you fight feeling and you become feeling. All you have to do is forgive and relax. Fear is a black horse; you never know when it will show up. You can't prevent death. All you have is fifty percent control, so live fifty percent to the fullest. Exercise one hundred percent of your fifty percent.

I'm a spiritual me; I'm a material me. There is always that dialectical relationship. Never abandon your conscience and kindness. Never abandon your kindness to yourself. Unlock the steel box and rescue your child innocence. Don't force a mold on your spirit. Fun should be spiritual fun. Fun should be what entertains your spirit. Exercise the spirit. Spirits that are not exercised haunt you, to get out. Enjoy the flower and respect the mud. Don't use another person's idiom; entertain your spirit.

You can't always go to the closet to reference your book, so, you must commit to know *Tao,* in your heart at all moments. The intelligent spirit absolutely wants you to know the truth. You have to merge the *Shi Shen* (intelligent spirit) and the *Yuan Shen* (original spirit). Merge in to *Tao.* You can't play God and you can't be afraid of God. An actively engaged life must be learned, so that, you be passively engaged without attachment. Virtue is true to self, so that it can be true to others.

Our intuition connects with the universe. We use our body to know the phenomenon, to know the world. The book, *Tao Te Ching*, uses an ultimate truth to describe humanity. You do not always need to know how something happened. "It just it." Try to understand the three treasures: conscience, mercy and forgiveness, to release the blockages. Embrace the devil to help the devil to initiate the love within. We want an organic spirit, with no polluted ground and no polluted seed. The "seed" is your *Xing* or essential nature. Sometimes, in church, there are organic seeds, but the heart can be polluted. Every problem can be solved with the three treasures of *Tao*. Possess kindness and love. Are you kind to yourself? Look deeply into your heart. Are you doing something professionally, or from your heart? You do things for humanity because you have love in yourself. You have a God in your heart-conscience; which is what embraces the devil. If you do not love yourself, you will be vulnerable, and can't embrace the devil. *Tao* is a Selfish *Tao*. You do not need a gun to kill the devil. In the ancient scriptures, they used analogies a lot to give the essence of *Taoist* teaching. "Look outside, there is no object; look inside there is no heart". My Master *Li* said, "Dance with the devil. Dance with all the negativity without judgment."

Chapter 41

Be Special and Want to be Special

God gives everybody a fair opportunity, intelligence and material, the material to create a successful life. You are a special human. To live is simply a gift from the universe. Many people are waiting for God to save them in all their lifetime, hoping that God will knock on the door and deliver the gift to their doorstep. Understand that each and everyone are unique and special. You will cook the best dish with whatever you have in your kitchen. That is the best dish that you can make in your life. Once you realize that you are special, you have to want to be special. Take action to create a true self with satisfaction and confidence. You must learn to open the door to get the gift. Rather than wait for the arrival of the gift.

Process # 33: Write down something about yourself, something that you absolutely have to share with another person.

It won't kill you when you make a mistake. Look at the mistake, and learn from it. Western culture tells you that you must pay for your mistakes. Why not just learn from them? Don't possess mistakes. Don't suffer from mistakes. Create a new fantasy for your life! Call it, "second-life.com." Be open to create someone you always wanted to be. If you can do two personalities, then you can do three. If you can do three, then you can do ten thousand. Go into your spiritual fantasy world. Unless you try and practice, you will never know that you can do it. How many costumes can you create for yourself? Multiple characters mean multiple wisdoms, multiple fears, and multiple capabilities. The same ingredients are capable of making many different tastes. Relearn to be imaginative. Relearn the ability to believe. Relearn the ability to act. These will all occur if you dare to live in a new character and be flexible. You can live ten thousand characters. Be special! Be a *Taoist* schizophrenic! Say, "I am flexible."

No matter what the gift you have been given, and how you interpret it, you should treasure it. Contemplate the gift to understand it. This is your true spirit, your original spirit. Look at it dialectically, from many sides. Does this home that we visited represent home? Is it your home, or the home of wisdom? Determine whether the gift is spirit wisdom or physical.

If you want to dream, why bother to dream small? Don't limit God's capability to provide the gift. Never downgrade the gift. God has capacity for unlimited wealth in his gift. Don't limit the power of the gift that God has given to you. This gift is all that you need. God gives to you whatever it is that you wish for. You can only interpret each moment. Attach to your gift. It is a magical gift. This magic will raise the boat. When you need a gift, rub the genie lamp.

"The crane stands alone among all the roosters and chickens." Once again, this is boring! Dragon men fly in the sky. Warrior men go to the battlefield. If you think you are somebody, then you are meant to do something. Don't compete with others. You can't compare and show how successful you are within this one room. The world is much bigger. There are so many unknown challenges waiting for you. Why do you worry about being so special in this moment for others? You say you are spiritual? That you are special? Then prove it! If you are a crane, stand among the cranes to show how special you are. Do you have the vision that you can have the whole ocean to swim in? Take it outside. Take your vision out of your limited house. You don't need to compete with your little community.

Yuan Shen, the original spirit, is so very big. Do not put yourself into a little box. Don't play with a ping-pong ball under the table. You know that you are limited there. You know that your ability is completely being limited. You limit your own ability, and yet you see yourself as powerful. Come out from the bottom of the well to see the sky. Don't limit the sight of your vision, and the ability of yourself to fly. Always understand, that your vision is limited by your current intelligence of the world. Also, always know your own limitations. Don't pretend that you are good at something that you are not. So many of us guard our ego, we guard our weaknesses. A strong human is not afraid to show the weakness, and is always self-entertaining. Be willing to give people compliments. When you give a complement to others you give yourself one, if you don't do this, you lose the respect of others. Be humble. Say you don't know. It's to your advantage to learn when you don't know. Do not be afraid to tell a joke about yourself. Do not be afraid to show your weakness to others. If others laugh at you, it is because of their own stuff to clean up. Be compassionate to have a conversation. This preserves your dignity. This is wisdom!

Once you identify the needle in the steel rod, make sure you have passion for yourself. Be willing to make change and make that change immediately. We are all on the battlefield, searching for food. There is always time for you to take a pause and to take care of the wound. You are better able after taking care of the wound. As you become wiser, your vision gets bigger.

The tiger is king of the animals on the mountain, but it is a pussycat in the meadow. When the tiger is in the meadow, he can be put to shame by dogs. Why? The tiger is meant to be in the mountains. Running uphill it excels to be fast. But they can't run downhill, so in the meadow, the tiger can be outrun. Understand both potentials and both possibilities—the potential to be king and not to be king. Then, you will understand where you are supposed to be and where you are not supposed to be. If you are a tiger, be in the forest. When the tiger is not in the forest, the monkey becomes king. When a powerful figure is not present, lesser figures jump out. If you have a wolf tail, you can never cover it and pretend that you are a sheep. So show your wolf tail. Your nature is your nature.

Treasure what you have in this moment. Treasure your gift from God. You have it for a reason. You are your own gift. Respect is a gift. Be your true self. Wear your own shoes. Don't try to walk like the people of *Hang Dan*, or you will forget how to walk and end up having to crawl home!

One of the four most beautiful women in China came to a riverside to wash her clothes. She shamed the fish with her beauty. Even flowers feel shame around her, and close in her presence. She is so beautiful! There was another girl who wanted to be so pretty like her. So this girl mimicked the woman in all her beauty, but in the process, she scared everyone away. In the end, a wise man said to her, "Why can't you just be yourself? You are pretty as you are. Everything about you is different from her. How can you pretend to be someone you are not?"

"Be yourself, everyone else is taken," said Oscar Wilde. There is an extra-ordinary someone inside each of us! Can you find it? Discover that someone. Trust that he or she is there! A complete human is ordinary and extraordinary at the same time.

Process #34: "I'm too sexy." Do a sexy dance in front of a mirror every morning. When you do this, you will never have to look for affirmation from another person.

Chapter 42

Allow the Flower of the Heart to Blossom

All the desires and emotions are like a smelly mud. How can you walk in the mud without getting smelly and dirty? The lotus extracts its nutrition from the mud. Likewise, wisdom comes from everyday life experience. Past life experiences can only present opportunity for today and the future. We don't need to have fear of living or dying. Learn to be ordinary and enjoy being ordinary. This will make you extraordinary. Fill your heart with joy, hope and passion for life. Nurture your heart with conscience, mercy and forgiveness. Joy will blossom like a lotus flower. Live in the present by walking out of the shadow of your past. It is always better, to live in the sun, than in, the shadow of the cave.

We get so confused and so tired with everyday life that we forget about the true purpose of life. Every day the spirit is drained. Deep down, at the bottom of your heart, you know the purpose of your life. The devil looks for the fake, complicated heart. God looks for the simple, truly sincere heart. Be willing to be ordinary and that is how you will become extraordinary. Then you are servant of all!

Return to simplicity. Simplify your complicated heart. Dust off your present heart, and unlock your true heart. Give yourself the opportunity to deliver the "Gold Mountain" from *Tao*. If you open your heart, the expedited delivery from God will come. It is always there, every day. Make yourself available. Find the mature child in you. Have the sparkle in your eye and trust. A strong physical and spiritual person can construct family wealth and personal wealth. If you are not crazy enough then you are not successful.

Find your head, and your heart, to find your direction. Find your motivation for success. Stupid people look for perfection. Your true heart, the true ingredient in the flower, has been shut off long ago. You have locked the door of the true heart. Give yourself a chance to turn deep inside to rediscover that true heart. Open the heart to receive the gift from God. Many people complain about others, they complain that God is not returning to them. A fake heart is not capable to receive from God. If you don't feel happy, there is no reward. Go back to your heart to pop the bubble around it. Tragic pain, and judgment against someone, can prevent you from getting there.

Emotion and judgment are merely nutrition for the devil. To sing the same song of God you have to be energetically compatible.

Holding onto pain, emotion and ego, to justify the reason to point a finger, is the well of the devil. When you point a finger you only become a slave to that person, feeling like a victim and wanting to persecute him or her. By becoming a slave, you prevent yourself from getting a reward. Free yourself from the slavery of emotions and judgments. After thirty days, whatever you hold onto becomes meaningless. Finding joy in your heart is true enlightenment.

Rediscover your meaning for existing and how you should live. What is the true life for you? What are the true wish and the true intent for your life? Find your sincere heart. God validates the sincere heart. Reconfirm and listen to your heart. Cleanse, adjust, cultivate, protect, preserve and rest it. Can you live in your own dream, without trying to please others, without becoming a victim? Sometimes you must join forces with somebody, rather than to persecute him or her, in order to get what you may want. Again, *Mengzi*, a disciple of Confucius, said, "Among the three people who walk towards me, one is my teacher!" You can always learn from someone, but your heart must be open to receiving. In order to become an extraordinary "I" you must allow your ordinary "I" to join you. Think, "I am a little wildflower in the desert that is thirsty for water." You are able to learn from everybody. Some people ask to receive, but then they persecute themselves and others for having received. If you think that you are perfect, then you are imperfect. When no intelligence exists, we return to *Tao*! Learn to receive, and then appreciate what you have received.

Be responsible for your own subconscious thoughts. "If I lack self worth, then, I will require others to prove themselves." Everybody is smart, including me. Be true to yourself and respect your own gifts. Don't wear someone else's shoes. Instead, find the shoes that kiss your feet. You do not want to have regrets. Harmony is the balance of perfection and defects. There is one teacher among every three people that you meet. Be willing to receive, and be willing to give. If there is a desire, then, there is always a product. Emotions always come with a product. Never say never! We are a strange and conflicted mind. You must be an ordinary human before you can be extra-ordinary. Respect the mud and then you will enjoy the lotus flower! The lotus is a product of the mud. True enjoyment means enlightenment!

Master *Li* said, "Once you are a diamond, you are always a diamond." True spirit cannot be covered by mud. Don't be lazy. Flush it with pure water and the diamond will shine. What you bring to the last breath determines your next journey. I hope that before I die, before my last breath, I can say that I have no regret. The blossom of the tang flower[7] only appears for one day, and the blossom only opens at night. When it blossoms the whole house smells fragrant. But when you get up in the morning it is gone.

---

[7] Night Blooming Cereus

The immortal, *Iron Crutch Li*, was from a highly educated family. He did not want to be a government official, and he did not want to pay attention in school. Instead, he would skip school to look for hermits in the mountains. One day he me met *Lao Tsu*, who was the first of the "Eight Immortals." *Lao Tsu* transferred alchemy to *Iron Crutch Li*, and as a result, *Li* achieved a breakthrough. *Iron Crutch Li* then proceeded to practice for fifty years, achieving a certain level of immortality. A faithful servant went with *Li*, to guard his body while he went into a stage known as hibernation. Li had asked the servant to watch over his body for seven days. *Lao Tsu* came to *Li* and guided him on his spiritual journey. On the sixth day, the servants' mother became very ill and was dying. The mother wanted to see her son one last time. So he struggled with what to do. Show loyalty to his parent, or to his master? It had been six days, and Li had not returned to his body from cultivating, so the servant decided to bury him as dead. In Chinese culture, loyalty to the parents is number one, and loyalty to the master is number two. When *Li* came back, there was no body for him to enter. He looked for a body and saw a body that had just died, so he entered it. When he looked at his reflection in the water he saw that he was very ugly and crippled. *He laughed and* then had a breakthrough. It is not about the form, detach from form, live to be a master.

You need to resolve your past. Dig out of your subconscious. If you only superficially clean up, it is hard to get into a deep stillness. Cleaning up the old will help you to achieve higher levels. Face your ego and face those that you have made errors with. Your parents have their own destiny. Can you go into your heart and see what errors you have made? This life is about relationships and love. Love is the best quality for material life, but emotional attachment is the worst quality for immortality. Emotional attachment is a lethal poison. You have to adjust the need for giving and receiving. Material is in both giving and getting.

The "three treasures" are what we use—conscience, mercy and forgiveness. Heal yourself and increase your connection to spirit. To give and receive love is human. Love can kill, and love can nurture. Do you carry the "treasures?" If not, that is your behind. Go into your soul to commit one hundred percent, truthfully. Then you will find the ultimate *Tao*, the "selfish *Tao*." Alchemy is like walking on a tightrope. It is much harder if you have baggage to carry. There is only one way to go forward. You need the 3-Ds—discipline, dedication and devotion–and no garbage. The southern gate is hot, heavenly fire. Every day I bring my head lower than my heart, ego lower than the soul.

We are pure pre-heaven *Yang* when in our mother's womb. We breathe from the umbilicus and there is no post-heaven energy. Only the eight extraordinary channels exist. It is dark, fire is below water and we have unconditional love from the mother. First you produce the best quality of human life, then you can refine. You have to let go when you cross over the line. That is how you balance life and immortality. *Tao* and virtue are behind the "three treasures".

What is the best for you? What is the blueprint? Have the best conscience and then follow the blueprint. Mercy gathers the materials and forgiveness is the tool. Every day you play the triangle game: victim, hero and persecutor. You always have to put the show on when you walk out of the house. Play the game playfully! You are one step away from happiness, and one step away from misery. There is one thought and one choice to make, to love or to hate. Take chocolate lightly, and enjoy it when you have it. Do not force yourself into the game; rather, celebrate it. Enjoy all the differences with your wife, friends, family and acquaintances. The more that you persecute, the more it will kick back. Softness overcomes hard; mercy is the water. Be soft like water. Softness is the application of the *Tao*.

During the *Tang* Dynasty, there was a prime minister in China, named *Wei Zhen*, who had told the king, "Water can carry the heaviest boat; it also can flip the boat over." When the prime minister died, the king said, that he had lost his mirror. You have to use the three treasures as a mirror in life, and also as a weapon. Rejoice every time you experience emotions and you will see the results.

Part VI:

Can I Get Home?

Chapter 43

Surrender Your Heart

My master told me, "As long as you still have one breath, you are capable and able to find a way of returning home." Once you are willing, and allow yourself to surrender your heart and your spirit to *Tao*, then your *Yuan Shen* will lead you to a right master. The master who will lead you to discover the master within, awakening the dragon master within and eventually bringing you back to the ultimate home of immortality.

Can I get home? Of course you can get home. The point is, that in Taoist practice we very practically point out the way or technique of cultivating the human body to unite with the spirit. In other words, we are giving the most fundamental, practical and authentic technique from the ancient times to today. Alchemy has followed lineage training, to give a way to explain the theory and technique for each and every one of us to learn how to get home. Every religion, each from a different angle, tries to explain how to get home. Mostly they are a fantasy and illusionary way. A broken car can't run ten thousand miles. You have to have a supersonic jet to get to heaven. A broken physical body can never carry an immortal's spirit. So, we give the reader practical techniques to cultivate eternal life. Understand essential nature. Cultivate the physical body and cultivate essential nature of the mind through a very practical way. Uniting entails the two parts. How great the saint and sage are. The saint and sage are not equal to the immortal, however. The saint and sage come back to reincarnate again. They are not equal to God or the immortal in heaven. Until the human understands the technique to cultivate immortality, they only gain an ability to find the gateway to immortality. Can I get home? Yes, you can get home! The way to get home is by uniting the mind and body. Don't just focus on talk; rather, focus on walking the talk.

Chapter 44

Cultivation between *Xing* and *Ming*

    Xing and *Ming* are concepts of internal alchemy in *Taoism*. *Xing* is essential nature, or the wisdom of the original spirit. *Ming* is eternal life, a physical material life. In *Taoism*, we emphasize cultivating *Xing* and *Ming* together. Do not prefer one above the other. Be compassionate and forgiving, cultivate your virtue to the extreme, like a saint or sage; or perhaps a living Buddha. But you still are not able to become a true immortal without cultivating a perfect physical life along with essential nature. Most religions emphasize cultivating the spirit over the body, but how many become immortal in their life journey? When you cultivate *Xing* (spirit) and *Ming* (body) together, a perfect physical body and mind will then nurture a wise spirit. Man is united with heaven as one. You then, have every possibility to get back home!

Xing is essential nature, pre heaven spiritual energy. It is the most important component for reversing life and returning to stillness. *Ming* is eternal life, post heaven energy. It is the vehicle for the return to *Tao*. Without *Xing* and *Ming*, return to *Tao* is not possible. One cultivates *Xing*, to process *Ming*. The person is the vehicle for returning to immortality. One must purify the spirit to become organic. *Tao* provides three opportunities for enlightenment in life. This book presents a principle for changing life.

In China, the dragon is the mystical animal that brings peace and harmony. But in western philosophy, the dragon is seen as an animal that destroys the world and needs to be slain. In a sense, the black dragon is the western dragon that destroys the world. We haven't yet come to terms with it. The black dragon needs to find the white dragon to forever merge and become the void. Western religion sees life as sinful and tortured. Don't let your emotional black dragon bring you down. The third minute, is the merge between the dragons. The dragon of *Tao* is the merge.

Xing is the black dragon, and *Ming* is white dragon. The first step is to find the black dragon, to attract the white dragon. The sixth sense is the merge of the five senses: sight, touch, sound, smell and taste. The five senses together equal the black dragon and the sixth sense is the white dragon. Evil dragon? Immortal dragon? There is no looking back! Every step is *Tao*.

The glue that you form is as a group. Each human's lineage is still here on this earth. Immortality comes with several aspects to work on. *Xing* is the mental. *Ming* is the alchemical. Virtue speeds the process up by collecting bonus, so to speak. You can create extra bonus through charity. However, that cannot be your reason for doing charity. The charity is done for charity's sake, not because you desire to become immortal. If you know who gets your giving, then, it is not charity. It's your ego. You should not think of doing good deeds. Rather, they should come from the heart. The receiver and the sender of charity are not known to each other. Small becomes big, and the straw boat collects the arrows.

You lose spiritual power with stress. Spirituality in *Tao* is *Xing* and *Ming*—the spirit and your body. Western spirituality many times is intellectual, or only *Xing*. We sit with our spirit in our body. Cultivate physical health to enrich the spirit within. For immortality you must return to the womb. The middle *dan tian* is post-heaven activity. You stop the post-heaven breath to circulate pre-heaven breath. When a baby is born, and has the first cry, the *Xing* rises and the *Ming* sinks. The *Shen* rises and the body sinks.

Chapter 45

Go Beyond Yourself,
Man Will Overcome the Heaven

Self and selflessness make a true self. People are stuck in the mud all their life. They try to resist and blame the mud. This only leads to digging deeper into the mud. Break the illusions of life to understand the true meaning of the "I." This will enable you to go beyond the self and selflessness. Then, you will find that the coin has a third side. A wise person does not have limitations of the self. He, or she, does not have a need for the self, yet, has a need to return to immortality. He, or she, combines the white and the black dragon, to form the third side of the coin. Then, there is no need for desire or attachment to the material self. You are able to let go of time and space, to go beyond time and space. A healthy, strong and happy longevity, plus a wise spirit, enables him, or her, to go beyond the limitations of the human life. You have the power to be in charge of your own life beyond a physical reality. "My life is in my own hands," is a slogan of Taoism. My master's living story proved the existence of living immortality. The third side of the coin is the mystical, physical door to immortality. It is wisdom that allows us to see the two sides, and to find the third side of the coin.

As you drown yourself in the pond of mud, remember, as long as you are able to have two fingers out of the mud, you can learn how to grab hold of your own hair and pull yourself out. "I am who I am," is equal to, "I am becoming who I am becoming." *Tao* and God are just names that we use to entertain ourselves. *Tao* is not religion. *Tao* that can be taught is no longer the eternal nature of *Tao*. We use the name only for our own entertainment. Each generation is just another form of the dragon. First, you have to stick with what dragon is. Stick your butt to it! We're riding the black dragon today; all the while we are exploring the white dragon. Eventually, the two dragons merge to become one dragon. The merge of the dragons is stillness. Merging into the balance is what creates the void. The void returns to *Tao*.

The dragon is the water. You ride it like you would ride a wild mustang. You need to have goals, but be flexible when pushing through life. Emotions are like a steel wall. You let the wall form because you give in to what you see. Even if you give in to only fifty percent of the emotion, it is still a steel wall. Everyone has a little darkness inside of the heart, you just need to unlock the door and let the sunshine in. Passion and mercy for life will encourage you to unlock the door. The key is within. You must be willing to take the key out. You don't need a hero to rescue you! Stop being the victim. When you carry the pain of childhood, you still assume that pain. You can be more than one character in your lifetime. First pretend to be someone you want to be. Then be that person. You must walk outside the box with another costume. How many of you are willing to be a multiple personality?

It is never too late to create wealth. God always has enough wealth to give. Am I the one to receive the Gold Mountain? You are not ready to open the door when you are still dancing with the devil. Would you learn spirituality from a poor

Master? Clearly, this Master does not have a gold garden. Intent is not in the right place. Man can occupy by day and night, but only God can verify the true heart. Always remember, you are with God. You can enjoy your infection, but I don't have to be infected, I am not obligated to feel guilty.

Chapter 46

Choose the Road of No Return

Cultivating stillness, for immortality, is the greatest mission in life. It takes discipline, trust, loyalty, determination and dedication. Cultivating immortality is like balancing on the high wire. With every step, there is the danger of falling off. Every step challenges the greatest fears. But the road you choose has no return. Each step you take leaves a deep footprint. It, ultimately, brings you the greatest reward in life. Once you set up the goal, for cultivation in immortality, I am sure that you are capable and able to get home.

"Stinky bull nose," is when the bull locks his four feet and refuses to budge. He never moves. Be stubborn in your belief of these principles. Stinky bull nose is a good name for a *Taoist* practitioner. The spirit never lies down. The spirit maintains its dignity of survival. In practical terms, however, if a robber comes in and orders you to kneel down, you kneel down to preserve life. Who will build the temple if you get yourself shot? You must be willing to be flexible. If, at any moment, you find something not to be true to you, then change. Don't be truly stubborn!

There's a pity party in hell and nothing but freedom in heaven. The practice of *Tao* is a one-way street. There is no looking back. Once you reach *Tao*, then, you are free to go back, should you so choose. You practice wisdom as you walk the tight rope. The bamboo pole in hand represents balance. You also practice one hundred percent purity, flexibility and life softness, which is application of *Tao*. You are walking the rope in the sky. There is only one direction to go. Never chime the symbols of retreat. Beat the drum of advance. Don't be the frog in the well, be the bird in the sky. Your motivation must be for self, but your motive must be to serve *Tao*.

Life is a stream. Never stop the flow. Trust and believe the beauty of mankind. Trust in *Tao* that you will never die. Have faith in God. You have a goal to live, have faith in that goal. Never question your goal. Love can bring power and love can bring poison. Love wisely! Believe in love and have faith in love. *Tao* will always bring a savior to your life. Never have a dying moment, even though it may look like dying. Have faith in *Tao*. During my three months begging on the streets, there was a time when I was cold and near death. It was at that moment, an old woman, even though she was wanting, stopped and gave me two hard-boiled eggs. Trust that the old lady will bring two boiled eggs. Embrace the end of your journey with a smile. Take with you the joy of faith. The only thing you carry with you in your journey is peace, joy and faith in *Tao*.

The lonely *Tao* is a one-way street. There is no return back. Once you know what it is, be on your way and don't turn back. You can fool the world but don't fool your spirit. A warrior is dead when he turns around to look at his wife and child, as he enters the battlefield. You can understand *Tao* only when you become the dragon. In life, only beat the drum, never hit the cymbal.[8]

No cage is big enough to cage the dragon. You can step back twice, if you are pushed on, but on the third time, don't be afraid to show the tiger's claw. Don't ever touch a tiger's butt! A true warrior is like a tiger; it will bite you. Don't let your butt be touched. When somebody starts to kiss your ass, be alert. It's a sugarcoated bullet.

Everyone is unique, so, do not copy others. You have to live your own life. "I am the messenger of *Tao*." Walk onto the battlefield with confidence; retreat from the battlefield with pride. Be consistent with what you believe and walk the talk. Never compromise your own integrity. When someone shows you a short cut to God, know that it is the devil in front of you. There is never a short cut! You have to work on it. There is no free

---

[8] From ancient warrior time the drum has represented the charge and the cymbal was retreat.

lunch and no free ride to heaven. You have to work on it each moment. Only those who ride the mystical hidden dragon can reach the heaven. That is why I say, "Be consistent in what you believe." Human nature is very vulnerable and weak. Are you able to stay with what you believe and walk the talk? I will always pray for you to be consistent with your belief and to not have to switch paths so often. Give yourself three to five years of consistent *Taoist* practice, using other paths as references in your library. The only thing you need to know is that *Taoist* philosophy encompasses every religion. Follow one frequency to follow your own channel. If you continually shop around, you are on a pathetic short-circuited channel and nothing can enter. Use your three materials of body, mind and spirit to build your own supersonic jet to heaven. Do not compromise the quality of these.

Chapter 47

Nurture the *Yuan Shen* to Perfect the *Shi Shen*

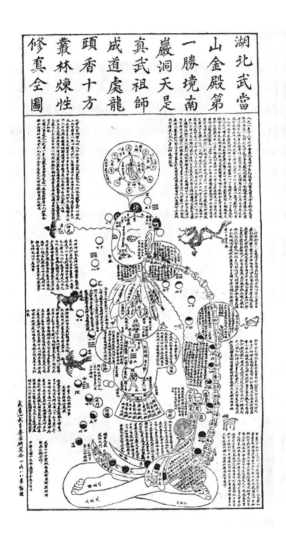

People accumulate their intelligence during their whole life journey. The attachment to the material life makes the imbalance between the *Shi Shen*—intelligent spirit—and *Yuan Shen*—original spirit. They are in constant struggle. Learning practical *Taoist* philosophy helps to balance the intelligence, allowing you to, eventually, break through the illusion to understand *Tao*. This makes the *Shi Shen,* or intelligent spirit, come to perfection, leading to enlightenment. It requires united *Xing* and *Ming;* cultivation practice and *Taoist* healing methodology such as: Tai Chi, *Qi Gong,* meditation, internal alchemy and *Kung Fu.* Through cultivation, you will eventually rediscover the common affinity between *Yuan Shen* and *Shi Shen,* allowing you to merge into the immortal world.

In all Chinese history, *Pan An* was the most handsome man. He was also very virtuous, like a saint. The immortals wanted to test him, to see if he was the one for heaven. So they sent a beautiful woman down to him. *Pan An* was sitting under a tree meditating. The woman from heaven, who was absolutely beautiful in all senses, came to the tree to seduce him. He did not move. She sat on his lap and he still did not budge. He did not even think of her as a temptation. His heart and soul were on an immortal journey. Temptation is not about resistance; rather, it is about why you even recognize it as temptation in the first place. The material is not at fault. The beautiful woman is not at fault. Why do you even have the need to look at this as temptation? This is an extremely important philosophy for meditation. When you experience extreme sexual arousal during meditation, no sage in the world can protect you from this sexual desire. The temptation is not there, so there is no need to entertain the desire. There is no particular technique that allows you to deal with temptation. You must walk the talk! This is an ingredient of *Jing* transmuting to *Qi*.

There are examples of these concepts presented in the Bible. Moses with the commandments on the tablets represents our conscience. The Red Sea is equal to the cycle of birth. Jesus in the desert for forty days and forty nights does not even recognize the devil as the devil or the temptation as temptation. There is no need for an arrow to protect from desire or for a gun to kill desire. It's about letting go of the need for desire! I have something better, my spirit knows. Don't think about the end of the road. Instead, think about each and every step along the way. Leave a deep meaningful footprint in each day.

To keep your cat claws sharp, look up into the sky at the clouds and see figures, animals and images in the clouds. This is the logic and illogic. Nature is your best master. It can enlighten you.

There is an advance time method; it is how my Master *Li* found me. At six years of age, my Master *Li* picked me up. She was one hundred years old at the time, in 1972. She couldn't travel thousands of miles, so she asked the *Kung Fu* master to travel to get me. The distance is the same as that of Kansas to Florida. The *Kung Fu* master traveled on train, foot and donkey. He had an exact description of me, as given by Master *Li*, the day, hour, location and dress. She described my hat, my bare feet and the green collar of my jacket. Outside the temple near my birth home there was a river flowing and the Kung Fu master practiced *Tai Chi* by a tree. I saw the branches shake on the tree and ran over. "Take me with you," I said. The *Kung Fu* master replied, "I have been looking all over for you!"

Every day, ask yourself, "Am I active or passive?" As you sit here, your ancestors access you. This is passive. But when you feel the joy, you are active. This is energetic incarnation flow. Always remain accessible to your own lineage. We synchronize with energies in the space we inhabit. When we meditate, we can access past and present spaces, events and people. From illogic to logic, from logic to illogic how do we access? It is through meditation, *Qi Gong, Tai Chi* and alchemy. These synchronize your physical frequency with spirit frequency. These practices tune you. These practices synchronize the body, mind and spirit. This gets you to cross over the channel. This is the mysticism that brings you from the world of *Yin*, to the world of *Yang*. A lot of the access happens in the middle, in between the worlds. To really see, you must be diligent and disciplined in the practices. But also, be devoted to your own life purpose. You will see!

In time, this process becomes automatic. Practice consciously. Then there will be no wall and no boundary. We choose. We are the ones who choose the separateness. If the choice is by logic you create separateness, then only logic flows. You become logic. We are taking the cosmic *Tao* and bringing it to the individual. Through practicing logically, you will attain the illogical. Then, you realize you no longer need to search because it is in you. Then, you have the technique to cross the boundary. Logic keeps us separate. When you realize there is no separation, then you realize, "I am one with God".

All of the techniques: *Tai Chi, Qi Gong, Kung Fu* and meditation are to get you to do nothing. You need to correct your physical imbalances. True alchemical practice also includes dietary approaches. They are used before practicing complete fasting. In the beginning, humans eat regular food. When we are moving into the "extraordinary human realm," a diet helps. Then, we are moving towards being an immortal. First, the earth follows the solar sun cycle clockwise. Later, you follow the moon lunar cycle counterclockwise and you eat sparingly. Everyone will have different responses in the *Dan Tian*. This depends on your level of *Jing*, your general health and other factors. *Nei Guang* means, "inner observation." *Tu Na* means, "breathe out, breathe in," the hard fire and gentle fire technique for meditating. *Jing Zuo* translates to, "tranquility sitting." These three are alchemy. The right technique is also very important. Proper sitting comes under proper technique. Starting the practice with *Nei Guang*, "inner observation," cannot be done without understanding the *Tao Te Ching*. Understand virtue, as well as *Yin* and *Yang*. The spirit is *Yang* and the body is *Yin*.

A Man's body is *Yin* and his eyes are *Yang*. A woman's body is *Yang* and her eyes are *Yin*. Introducing the *Shen*, or original spirit, to the body is the most important. The first step is the most important! Have conscience, mercy and forgiveness. Combine *Yin* and *Yang* to find the whole, *Shi Shen* (mind) and *Yuan Shen* (spirit). Love to be positive. If you pursue the negative, you become it.

Chapter 48

Cultivate Internal Alchemy and Return to Home

Alchemical practice is a very secret and complicated cultivation method. It is scientific and efficient. Meditation methods help the ordinary person to attain the perfect physical health. It takes ten years to make one breakthrough, perhaps thirty to one hundred years to become immortal. Then, you no longer need a physical body as a carrier. You have the freedom to travel time and space. My Master *Li* lived to be one hundred thirty years old. She chose her own time and space to leave to the immortal world. This was witnessed by hundreds of people.

At times, we cannot access what we need to, because, we have blocked our power. You want to be able to access through the, "narrow entrance." You want to connect the spirit and grow wings to fly into the sky. Improving your spirituality through virtue, mercy, forgiveness and compassion are only the first part of the process. You really have to physically cultivate to become a "super-being". You are learning a secret to communicate with your spirit. Being a better person is the first level reward.

To meditate, sit on the floor with legs crossed into the "lotus" position. If this is not possible for you, then, sit on a chair with your feet flat on the ground. Sitting in the lotus position the left leg should be wrapped outside the right leg for men, and for women, just the opposite. Place the hands in front of the lower *Dan Tian* (approximately two inches below the naval), with the right hand cupped around the left hand (for males), and both thumbs touching just below the third finger on the left hand. The hand position is, once again, opposite for females. The tip of the tongue touches lightly onto the palate of the mouth. Females close the eyes lightly. Males should leave just a slight slip of light fall through. Take a cleansing inhalation and exhalation, and relax. Focus on a spot between the eyes and in front of the brain—*Zhu Qiao*. Imagine the sun rising, and on the next inhalation, bring the sun into the *Zhu Qiao*. The sun enters through the *Zhu Qiao*, or third eye. Internally, look down on the exhalation, as the sun drops to the lower *Dan Tian*. Continue this cycle of natural breathing and imagining the sun filling the brain and then the body with light. Should you lose focus do not condemn yourself, just gently bring yourself back to your breathing. Do this meditation, for up to an hour, twice a day early in the morning and before sleeping at night. We go through the conscious mind to get to the spirit. All actions in meditation should be without effort, without forced creation. If sensations arise, remember that, "It just it." Learn to see things without seeing. See without attachment. Hear without hearing. Feel without feeling. Practice with unconditional love.

The void is the body of *Tao*, but it is not empty. Follow your nature. Your essential nature needs to break through. The technique to break through has to be taught by an authentic master. Be a deep well of still water. Without peace you cannot find tranquility. Without dialectic relationships there is no tranquility.

The product of meditation is vaporized into energy. You are transmuting *Jing* to *Qi*.

Without achieving stillness, you achieve nothing. It is the most important step for obtaining longevity and immortality. It is the foundation technique. As you improve, cultivating *Qi* and transmuting it to *Shen*, you will never age. You form the "macrocosmic orbit." After one hundred days of meditation, the quality is much better and

Jing is transmuted to *Qi*. There is a new element in the body. You can feel the dragon swim in the body. The imagined dragon is transformed into the material dragon. Before the dragon comes though, you have to conceive and design it; and exercise the mind of *Tao*.

Formation of the first brick in the house is a wonderful achievement. Talk is cheap, so show me something! *Tai Chi* is a technique for moving the vehicle. *Tai Chi* is the art of *Taoist* philosophy. *Wu Dang* passes along the most fundamental and authentic tradition for *Tai Chi* and *Kung Fu* in China. In seven hundred years they have never given away this art for commercialization. It looks secret, yet it is very simple. It is very simple, yet very difficult. There are nine levels of doors to open. Traditional teaching used a lot of analogies and traps, so that there would be many layers of protection.

Ren Xian is a human immortal, and this gives you longevity. *Di Xian* is an earthly immortal, and *Tian Xian* is a heavenly immortal. You have to put the accessories together. As soon as you have created one *Yang* of energy, then, you have accomplished the first step. To transmute *Jing* to *Qi*, you will have sexual arousal without intent. When the arousal reaches the level of the San Francisco fire, then, you go to the fire drill. The cause of this sexual desire is different. It is not from human desire. When the fire shows up, you must use wisdom and intelligence. If the dam breaks, then, the dragon runs away. It takes thirty to sixty days to save up again. Patiently learn the dragon, and become the dragon. Then, you just know it. *Qi* is in the *Dan Tian*. Without harmony and centering, you have nothing. Having, and not having, both rise together. Raise energy from low to high, and then down to the *Dan Tian*, where the energy is deposited.

Cultivating stillness begins in part, with the daily practice of meditation. Set aside time to physically still the body and mentally still the mind, so that, you may begin to know your spirit. Meditation can come in many forms and may include meditation-in-motion techniques such as *Tai Chi*, *Qi Gong* and *Kung Fu*. Meditation-in-motion techniques encourage you to focus intently on the movements and breath of the body, quieting the busy mind. In tandem with meditation-in-motion techniques, the disciplined and dedicated practice of sitting meditation will, over time, cultivate stillness in the body and mind.

Cultivating is equal to returning to the motion of *Tao*. This is when the eye sees color, but does not take it in. It sees beauty, but yet, does not see it. If you have mind activity, then, your mind will deplete your essential nature. The mind is the worst thief that steals *Yuan Shen* (original spirit). The eye is a worse thief, when it comes to cultivating. The ear must hear and still, not hear. You are hearing, but not receiving the sound, not attaching to the sound. Although your spirit is aware of the sound, your mind does not rise in thought or intent.

Cultivation is when you see things and do not get attached. That is cultivating. Don't get attached! Cultivation is the principle of, how to drive the car. When one *Yang* comes, you are then, transmuting *Jing* to *Qi*. If you are not a skillful cultivator, it means that you do not have faith in *Tao*. When one *Yang* comes, if you don't believe in immortality, then you will easily give up. You will give in, or won't have the ability to notice it. When you are not paying attention, you won't be able to see the beauty of the flower. You know that *Jing* is already there, you must exercise the power of spirit. If you are not able to notice, you leak and lose energy. Returning is the nature of *Tao*. My life is in my own hands. The apple becomes very sweet after one hundred days. The goal is one hundred days of cultivating! Good quality brings good health and longevity.

One hundred days of practice; however, does not make you a God. Choosing fun for a day can destroy your spirit for a lifetime. Having said that; be willing to forgive yourself for making a poor choice, but resolve not to do it again. Take time to process mistakes, so that you will realize to never do it again. Possess the power of the will to make the true choice. You can devour the choice, or you can choose to let the choice make you retarded. Know that your master will make loving choices for you. However, don't retire your wisdom, devour your wisdom. Kiss yourself and make love to yourself. If you can't make love to yourself, then, your love for others will only be half designed.

The writers of the Bible knew the immortality concept. Jesus dying on the cross, with a thief and a murderer, represent the *Yang* and *Yin* merging into the cross. Jesus on the cross is the merge. "I die for your sins." If the human, intelligent self dies, then, the spirit lives. The blood is symbolic of *Jing* transmuting to *Qi*. "God my father, why have you forsaken me," means you have not forsaken me in the dialectic. The Red Sea spreading open represents sexual energy. One *Yang*! You can only see what you choose to see.

When meditating, if you feel a stream of electrical heat flash the face and it feels like ants crawling all over your face, then you are at a point of break through. You will feel a whirlpool of *Qi* circulating on top of your head. The three golden flowers are gathering at the head. You are transmuting *Jing* to *Qi*. *Jing* is returned to nourish the brain. The tube of the eyeball, is what, causes the spark. It shows up in front of the *Zhu Qiao* or third eye. Completely let go. It shows up at the *Jiang Gong* like a moon, or wisdom light. Spirit light lightens the empty heart. *Zhu Qiao* is the gateway for the spirits to come in and out. You must tie the wild horse tight to the pole. Cage the jumping monkey. The heartbeat can be lowered to three to seven beats per minute. Stay with *Zhu Qiao*, to forget about *Zhu Qiao*. The focus is to forget. If you use mind and intent to look for it, then there is manifestation. If you use no heart to stay with it, you fall into emptiness.

The *Shi Shen*, or intelligent mind, prevents us from breaking through. Maintaining the right technique is also very important for breaking through. Proper sitting is included under proper technique. Starting the practice with *Dao Yin* will help. The posture in meditation is very important. The spine must be straight, if collapsed, *Qi*, oxygen, and nutrition cannot get to the brain. The head needs to be engaged, pushing up, with the chin down slightly, so that the back of the neck is not blocked. Shoulders need to be down and slightly rounded. If they are up, it will block the flow of energy. The eyes look toward the tip of the nose to tie the wild horses to the pole. If the muscles are not trained, the eyes will move around and there will be distracting thoughts. Both hands are sealed. There should to be enough thumb pressure, and at the right place, to slow down the heart and blood flow. It "cages the monkey." The legs are best when in a full lotus position. This cuts the need for blood flow to the lower body, so that it goes to the head. It maximizes *Qi* flow. The blood needs minimum work, with maximum results. The organs need the most amount of blood, so they last longer. Always face east or south when meditating. Do not meditate in complete darkness, natural light is best. Build a foundation for cultivating yourself. Cultivate your mind and essential nature. Work on cultivating heart and mind, cultivating *Xing*. If you don't cultivate your essential nature, it can't survive. You have to let go of the post-heaven spirit and enlighten the pre-heaven spirit. If you do not cultivate the spirit, it will not become mystical. The spirit is like a pet; you have to cultivate it to do a trick. A pet fish is not happy if it is not cultivated. You must cultivate the spirit to make it alive. Only when you kill the *Shi Shen* (intelligent mind), can you activate the *Yuan Shen* (original spirit).

PART VII:

I Am the Master

Chapter 49

Leaving the Mountain

At the age of sixteen, my master thought that I was ready to leave the mountain; that I need to go into the world. All that I had learned in the temple was only thirty percent. The other seventy percent has to be learned and practiced during your life in the community. Until you go into the community, you are not a master. To practice immortality, you have to practice humanity first. It is called practicing humanity *Tao* before you practice heavenly *Tao*. As I was ready to leave, my Master *Li* felt confident that I was capable of leaving the mountain. But, my *Kung Fu*

master wanted to see whether I was really mature enough to leave. He had very special way of testing me, to see if I was ready or not.

It was a pretty chilly day, a cold day. The wind blew mist around the mountain. Master *Guo* brought me to a temple, called *Nan Yan* Palace, on a cliff. It was built over several hundred years ago. In the very beginning, around 1200 years ago, people had already been cultivating there. About 700 years ago, it became a temple. At this temple, there is a very special stone dragonhead that, projects out from a cliff. The dragon's head is maybe one and one half feet wide and projects about five feet out from the cliff face. An incense burner sits on top of the dragon's head. Legend says, there is an evil dragon below the cliff. When the *Zhen Wu* god came to the mountain to cultivate immortality, he decided to restrain this evil dragon. He moved a mountain so that it sits on top of the dragon. Now, it can no longer get out to do evil things.

When they built the *Nan Yan* temple on this cliff, they built the beam of the dragon's head under the temple, with the dragon's head sticking out from the cliff. The temple sitting on top of the dragon is symbolic of restraining the dragon. The stone dragon's head points directly to Golden temple, located at the highest peak of the *Wu Dang* Mountains.

Worshipers walk out on to this five-foot long stone carving to burn incense. It is said, if you can walk out and back in one piece, without falling, that you are most sincere and loyal. It is considered that the evil dragon is still alive, so if a person of no virtue comes to place incense in the burner the dragon becomes restless. It twists and turns, trying to knock the person, and their incense, down. Only those that have the greatest loyalty, sincerity and peace of the mind are attracted. If the mind is not peaceful or sincere, or if, in your life you have done some bad deeds, then the dragon might disappear under you. There is a five hundred to one thousand foot drop below this dragon. The older people say, that as late as 1950 many people died falling off from the dragon's head.

As I said, my test came on a very misty and cloudy day. Mist floated around the valley. With the floating mist and blowing wind, I could only see the valley on one side and not the other. The mist blew back and forth. It was very windy and the weather was not so good, making the situation a bit more frightful.

My *Kung Fu* master brought me to this temple site and said, "Okay, here it is. You go out and stand on the dragon's back in the Golden Pheasant Stand, in a one leg posture." It is a *Tai Chi* posture, where one leg stands and the other leg is in the air. The two arms spread apart, like a phoenix.

"You have to stand there at least twenty minutes," he told me. The test is to keep the mind still. If you can, you then become one with the universe, one with the stone, and one with the temple. You won't see the stone or the cliff. You won't see yourself. When you don't see yourself you don't have emotions, you don't have fears, you don't have concept and judgment; and so, you enter this grand void and this void becomes the *Tao* and you are the *Tao*. This is high-level achievement as a *Taoist* priest.

He said, "You go stand there. I'd rather that you shame me here at this moment, than to bring shame on me later in the community. I spent ten years training you in martial arts and if you don't pass, then I feel shame that I didn't train you well. You can die here, rather than go out and die in the community, or go out and disgrace the name of *Wu Dang* in history." After he made this comment, I felt a strong sense of responsibility and a lot of pressure. So you know, the first moments I went out, I felt my heart pumping. "Ten years of training so my master expects me to pass this test," I thought to myself. I of course, wanted to pass and show myself that I could do this too. With this kind of attitude, you go out and you start to feel your body swing and sway. A long ten years of training with alchemy and *Kung Fu* were at test. As soon as I started to pose, it took only five to ten seconds before everything disappeared in my mind. All of a sudden, I felt tremendous stillness. Everything became still in my mind. The wind was still, no longer did the cliff exist underneath, the clouds wrapped around like a comforter and the one leg was just like a root holding deep into the stone. I became a decoration of the stone, unified with the stone. After twenty minutes, Master *Guo* called me, but I couldn't even hear him. I was out there for over thirty minutes. After that amount of time I thought, "This is cool, can I stay a bit longer?"

Many people look for a master all of their life. Bowing, worshipping, and kneeling down to an "unknown" power. They give away their own strength, belief and self-respect to a master and are willing to become the slave of a master. *Tao* invites each and everyone to look for a "master within." You are, and capable to be, a master. *Tao* is an interesting concept. The more you think you get it, the more you lose it. You cannot describe it. You can only feel it. When you think you can feel it, that's when you lose it.

"I am the master." After you review all the previous chapters, the path of the master from within naturally appears in front of you. You do not need to spend all the money, searching the world for the secret. You don't need to worship this, or worship that. You don't need to worship anything exterior. No matter how many temples you have been through, no matter how many Sundays you have gone to church, no matter how many books you have studied, no matter how many workshops and lectures you have attended, there is no secret when you understand that, the master lies within. As the movie *Kung Fu Panda* says, "There is no secret ingredient in the secret ingredient noodle soup." My Master *Li* once said, "How many people do not understand the donkey? They are looking for the donkey, while riding on the back of a donkey. Riding on a donkey to look for a donkey." Immortal *Lu Dung Bin* says, "How many fools do not understand?" *Tao* is right in front of your eyes, stop searching all over. The God or Buddha is always inside your heart. You do not need to go outside to search for the masters, or to willingly become a slave of the exterior human. Discover the master from within.

You and I are both qualified to be the master. The question is, are you ready to be the one? Seeing is accepting that, "I am already the master." Every person has the master within. However, you have to unlock the steel box to let the master out. Ninety-nine point nine-nine percent of all humans live for other people. Very few people will live for themselves. In part, this is due to the influence of religions and culture that separate the God and the human. Making God into a separated ruler, so that humans are always below. This indoctrinates people to obey and worship the external. Look inside to find the master, and look inside to make God blossom! God is you. Throughout history, very few people dare to make this statement, saying, "I am the God." Saying, "I am *Tao*, I am the God, I am the master of mine own." Instead, you learn that you are not in charge of your life in most religions. In Taoism, we give the information to understand that you are in charge of your own life. Extend beyond the nature and beyond God. You are in charge of your body, mind and spirit.

We give techniques to remember who God really is, because without the proper amount of internal *Qi*, you cannot have the capacity to see a glimpse of God. The more you cultivate *Qi*, the more of God you see. The more you see of God, the more you see self as God. It takes *Qi* to have good clarity, to see the brightness and merge into God. Without cultivation, you cannot see the master within. The story of the Jade Emperor God, grinding a metal rod to a needle, illustrates the discipline needed, leading to good choice and change. He practiced forty-two years and didn't even notice that he had become a physical God.

Wisdom of *Tao* is not the intelligence. Wisdom of *Tao* facilitates intelligent actions, but intelligence is not *Tao*. Wisdom functions like intelligence, but intelligence is not wisdom.

When you work without fear, you need no armor to protect yourself. Passion and love are more powerful than any armor. There is nothing to be lost and so, you have nothing to lose. Do not apply a label to, or for others. Allow people to identify for them self. Eastern medicine works on the predicate of prevention. Western medicine waits for a problem to solidify and then works towards a cure. One works towards prevention of a problem and the other works towards cure of a problem.

Chapter 50

Look for the Master from Within

Those people who can help others to become a master are a true master. The master is there to serve, contribute, and to love. You do not need to look for a master from outside. You are born to be a master. We do not need to be making a master of others during our lifetime; the master is within. Return to the root of stillness, and you will discover the true master within. My Master once told me, "You have to be a fool riding a donkey, to look for a donkey."

There is only one thing to master and that is, "my self." Act like the character, put the costume on. One created two, two created three and three created ten thousand. Master your own costume. Always find the truth between truth and fake, truth and false. Be in between the true and false. The dragon is invisible but we are visible. Live and let live.

Be in between attachment and detachment, detach from truth and false, become the true one, achieve physical immortality. The essence of alchemy is *Yuan Qi,* equals organic spirit transforming the dragon. You must cultivate in stillness! Sexual arousal in stillness is the mother dragon finding the fittest dragon.

See and not see, know and not know. Detach, to nurture for nine months. In stillness and in the dark, detach and attach. All this energy is the dragon. From simple to complicated, always dialectical. A scholar may read ten thousand books and may intellectually know a lot of information, but he has not walked the talk. The true teaching is three words; "walk the talk". You must be the master of the dragon. Intent comes before *Qi.* *Qi* comes before the movement. You fight fire by going ahead of the fire. Lead the dragon, and then be the dragon. Master your dragon. You must give up the emotions, or you will just be an average driver. What stops you from leading your heart to where you want to go? If you know it, then guide it, master it, and be it. Guide your heart to your dream! Know and understand all your past mistakes and then you can overcome them.

If you want to fail, then you will indeed fail! Win in spirit and not in logic. Have no ego. You must possess spiritual winning, in order to have physical winning. A good blueprint always produces a good product. Have a good spiritual blueprint, follow that blueprint and you will build it; by doing so, you accept your spiritual wish. "Every dish I decide to cook will be the best dish," is the recipe for success. A silkworm spits silk into a cocoon that he can't get out of. He gets caught into his own web, tangling himself. You must untangle the web. You must not tangle yourself into a web. In order to unlock the lock, you must find the key. You are your own prisoner; therefore, "I am my own liberator. I am my own master! I am the master of my own!" This is the fire that keeps you alive. You are clinically suicidal if you cannot say this sentence. The more you say it, the more it will gain an electrical charge. "I can do it! I have done it!" If you say that you can't do it, then you are playing the victim role. Accept nothing but perfection in your spirit.

Your *Shi Shen*, intelligent spirit, needs to love the master within. *Shi Shen* does not need to be perfect. People who have low self-esteem will step on themselves and crap on themselves. I am the master of my own! I am not a slave! I am not a slave of my emotions, my self-esteem, or my community. I am not hungry for garbage! Everything that man desires for is worthless. If you do not have a strong foundation, then you will come crashing down. Live in the logical and the illogical at the same time. Never show the whole dragon. Detaching is the way to attach. Attaching is the way to detach. Saying, "I don't have a need," dialectically means, "I have a need for no need." You can't separate from the *Yin* and the *Yang*. Learn to live in the dialectical.

You must have to have a physical life before you can live in the immortal life. Life is both fiction and nonfiction, so allow yourself to be entertained. Don't be raped by yourself. Do something that expresses the spirit in your body as a whole. Life is as real, and not real, as it gets. Taoist logic says that you have to destroy existing concepts to build the concept of *Tao*. All you can do is keep your butt on the dragon. If your butt doesn't sit, well, then it is a fantasy! Being philosophical is not living! A master's goal is to see the making of another master in his students, so you must go beyond me. If a master can't produce a master, then he is not a good master. A master is merely a facilitator. It is when you hit the wall, that you must see yourself on the other side of the wall. If you give in to the obvious power, then you are restraining creativity. There is always something new that you can overcome. When you are ready to throw the towel into the ring, it is then that you must give it one more chance. Then, you will become the master, no longer a slave of failure. Give a *Taoist* finger to the concept of failure.

Think, "I am a dragon. There is not a big enough cage to contain me. There is no sky big enough to allow me to fly. No one can possess me. I am the master of my own!" Nobody has any right to say that, "I own you." It can be a very negative power to try to cage someone else's spirit. *Tao* can't be possessed. Cultivate in stillness and become master of your own. Do not, however, jump on the stage to become master. People are fearful of the unknown and this can be used to one's own benefit. Don't get side tracked for power and gain. Put out your most positive intentions to achieve the path of *Tao*. Don't allow negativity to push you all the way to the curb. Allow yourself to be pushed back two steps, but if pushed a third step, it is okay to show your claws. *Tao* will never abandon you, though you may abandon *Tao*.

The answers are always inside. You are a fool to ride on a donkey, and still look for a donkey. The spirit is always with you, but you always search outside for answers, asking others to guide you on how to live life. I am not your master. You are your own master. I am just a person fifty steps ahead of you. I am just the messenger. I am the tour guide. You always have had your master. You were born with it and you will always have it. If you know your life purpose, then you have already awakened your master within. I know the path. I have been here before. I am guiding you. I am like an old horse that knows the path. I have no intention but to take you there. I fish with a straight hook. Know that each one of you has awakened your own masters. It is my sincere hope that every one of you is able to preserve your master, as you preserve your own life. Go beyond material life events. This is the perfect Broadway Show! Once you join the club, you will have so much fun! Everyday put on your costume, at night take it off and return to your true self. Can you do it?

Heaven for *Yuan Shen*, or original spirit, is to live. Paradise is based on my understanding as a *Taoist* priest.

We all have to learn the skill. Use my guidance to create your own paradise, to create the ultimate paradise for your own spirit. Find the opportunities to reconstruct and return home. There is no absolute secret, or method, from your master. It is only absolute for each of us individually. I can only attempt to describe the feeling, taste, and look of it. Learn the principles, but in the end, it is still up to each of us to take the action to create it.

So often we are sidetracked by a certain reality, thinking that what we know, we know. Be brave to allow for another possibility to exist. Allow for that possibility to happen. You only need a fifty percent possibility; then, just one percent more makes it real.

Invite the spirit with you on your journey. You invite, and then persuade, it to fall in love with your body. But first, you must extend the invitation. If the invitation is not there, the spirit won't feel comfortable to enter. It won't feel welcomed. If the invitation is not sincere, then comfort and feeling of welcome is not there and so, the visit is short. If you are not sincere, then there is no spirit loyalty. The key to immortality is to access into spirit function, rather than human function. Always access illogical function, so that logic and illogic functions are being used simultaneously. It's about running on a different frequency. Be in the place of no desire and no ego. It comes from a place of stillness. Allow the spirit to travel at a different frequency, to be the guide of attaining the goal. Once you have *Tao* in you, and you use it, your potential is unlimited and pretty mystical.

The logical body follows behind the spirit. Your spirit always guides you in the right direction, but the body drags your feet. It takes you off focus and brings you to temptation. Entertain with your body, but never lose your spirit. Allow your spirit to walk ahead of you and guide you. Accept that the human body can be a dummy, but never underestimate the spirit potential. Whenever you function as a human, you experience all the human ego and emotion. It is okay to entertain them. Allow your self to be human, but mostly allow yourself to be a spirit. World peace comes from one place, "within." Be a Master! Make Masters. Then you can claim yourself to be a Master. Discover the "Master Within" by helping others to discover the Master Within.

Chapter 51

True Happiness is Freedom

At four years old, my parents were farmers. As farmers, we had a little land by the river. My parents were working there, at the side of the river, and I was there with them, playing by the river. There were reeds and vegetation by the river, but at the very edge of the river, it was very slippery. While they both worked, I had fun chasing after little crabs. They would run into small holes, and I would try to dig them out. While doing this, I slipped. It was summer; I slipped and slid right into the water.

Under water, I choked a couple of times and was afraid for a few seconds, but then, I felt mud on my feet and thought, "Oh, this is very soft." So, I forgot there was water. Immediately, I felt connected to the mud. My eyes opened, and I saw small fish and shrimp swimming. Instead of chasing crabs, as I had been on shore, I now chased the shrimp and fish, but they were pretty fast. My young hands reached into the mud for them. I crawled in the mud, chasing them. I saw some big clams and put them into my pockets, and then continued following the fish and shrimp. I seem to recall that there were a couple friendly shrimp and fish that guided me out.

Underneath the water, it was very bright and I saw the mud, shrimp and fish in front of me. They seemed pretty slow, but when I tried to catch them they easily swam away. I was underwater for at least a half mile. My ma told me that I was under the water for half an hour, and that all the people, the farmers, were helping to search for me. After twenty minutes they gave up. My Ma and Pa were sobbing and crying next to the river. When I ran up to them and said, "Ma and Dad what are you doing? Why are you crying?" they looked at me in shock. I told them, "I caught two clams." and then, they laughed and cried. I was soaking wet and covered in mud. For a moment, people screamed. Everyone thought I was crazy. They already thought I was special. This event only gave them more proof that I was special and mystical.

People asked how I survived under the water. Under the water, I merely felt like, "Just have fun."

Children love mud and play in the mud all the time, it is a natural thing. I didn't have fear. I didn't think of it as, being under water, and so, there was only joy. The shrimp and fish guided me out; if they went fast I went fast. I didn't think about breathing. Looking back, I didn't have the concept of death. In the water there is a lot of oxygen, so when you don't think about fear then your function like a fish. I did not know how to swim, that is why I crawled in the mud. It was very fun.

There are so many different levels of happiness in life. Some enjoy material happiness, fame and money. Others enjoy having nothing. Some say that they enjoy spiritual happiness; this is truly pathetic. And other people enjoy both, the material and spiritual happiness. None of the above is true happiness. It is just the shadow happiness. Having the ability to go beyond reincarnation, stop reincarnation and return to the immortal world is true happiness. Enjoying the absolute freedom of doing so is the true happiness. We are all capable.

An immortal has no purpose, yet an immortal has "all purpose." An immortal possesses complete freedom of all choices. Don't reserve your mouth. Listen when you talk. *Tao* is very freeing; it opens you to all choices, and no desires. It's about finding unity from polarity. Walk the talk. A mortal's purpose is to be happy! An immortal has no purpose.

You must walk the talk! Life is a vehicle and the purpose is to transport from spirit to body, back to spirit and then to *Tao*. In doing so, you liberate your whole lineage. Your whole lineage is upgraded. Life is upgraded. Immortality is a reflection of life. You can't drive a car by reading a book, and you can't learn to drive a car by only driving it once in a while. You must practice, practice and practice. Once you learn to drive a car, you can pretty much drive any car. Understand the goal! You are the one. Know that, "I am the one." Do not judge yourself. Do not give yourself excuses to not be me. If you are a human, then be a happy human. Make choices with virtue. Check out the movie "Needful Things" by Stephen King. If you have something that you are unwilling to give up, then the devil exists in you. This will prevent you from ever seeing a dragon. Only happiness will keep you alive and bring you back alive.

Process #35: Go ten years into the future. Fill your hopes into this future. All your today's hope, are now reality. Then look back from those ten years to today. Did you get to laugh at yourself? Look at all the accessories and how you shop for them. The structure is always there. You have it. It's the accessories that change. Your mind fools you about time and space.

Live beyond the reality, beyond the time. This is what makes a visionary person. Live in your dream. Today is the dream! So every day you are doing accessory shopping. It looks risky to others, but you are constructing. It can take ten years, but you are building it each day. Others may not understand, support or approve. Oh well!

History does not approve visionary people. Can you live beyond your own vision? I do.

Tao gives all power back to you, the human. All immortals came from human. They maintain another incarnation invisibly. This life journey is to give you a choice. You are in the middle. You can turn left or right. You choose. Looking at it in this way, the world is a figure eight. Understanding about the creation of the universe comes from *Lao Tsu, Tao* and Virtue. These come from the Precious Treasure, which comes from the Original Spirit.

Humans make a choice to know only a little. But when you invite in original spirit, it comes to you with total reunion and you are absolute power. This life is such a happy journey. We have so much to access. We have every treasure and skill. They are always available to us. All we need to do is access it. Take the treasures out one at a time and use them. Why limit your self? The immortal has unlimited power and skill. What I'm teaching you is, be human and be spirit. Be the best human and the best spirit. Live in spirit and entertain the human. Life is joy. Can you imagine living in unlimited joy?

Process #36: Throughout the day recite, "I am my own Master."

Whenever you feel unsettled practice a nightly prayer. The order is important; otherwise you make the prayer your own. Pray to the universe to bless the world.

Pray for your parents and ask for a blessing for them. Forgive your parents and ask for appreciation of them. Ask for them to live long and in peace. Pray for all the masters, the second parents. Give gratitude that they continue to guide. Pray for your family, your brothers, sisters and relatives. Pray for the local community. Pray for your own personal desire, your business, family, health and wealth. Ask for a partner if you don't have one yet and ask blessings for his or her family too. Finally, pray again to the universe. This prayer brings peace, glory and self-respect. You will feel great! Learn to pray to your own Master. Praying to your own universe is more powerful than praying to any God. Self-prayer is absolutely powerful. This is not being associated to any religion. Your master is most powerful, more powerful than God. This is your own original lineage. This is God!

Chapter 52

You Hold the Key to Happiness

Tao or God is inside your heart and spirit. In cultivating stillness, taste the joy of life. You are the only one to hold the key at the bottom of your heart, where the steel box has locked your heart. No one in the world can help you, unless you are willing to find the key to unlock the joy of your life.

You must maintain passion for life so that you don't persecute others, by giving up on yourself. It is then that you become someone. You must know your spiritual and personal identity, and never let go of it. Translate these principles into applications. In being strong, it is okay to allow yourself to be weak. If you want to live in an illusion, then you will be in a life of illusion all the time. You have been taught the technique, now it is up to you to implement the technique. Try to catch yourself when judging, because you are only hurting yourself by judging others. These techniques only work when you have conscience, mercy and forgiveness. When you win, then everybody wins. Develop three-dimensional observing. Kiss your butt and the butt of whomever it is that you are talking about. Small talk can really be big talk. Through invisible signs, you see the principle. All humans have passion for life. If both people win, then there is creation and grand harmony.

It's painful to have a tumor cut out, but you will heal once it is removed. If you don't cut the tumor out, you will die. One needle in the right spot and no second needle is needed. Actively engage, one hundred percent. Never regret. Be happy on your funeral bed. Don't wait for people to talk about you, talk for yourself. Life always presents you with a surprise! Find your tail. Never push your friends to the corner. If you choose with a hammer and knife you are murdering. Scratch but don't stab. Give others a fifty percent chance to awake; give your friends a fifty percent chance of being God. Don't push your enemy to a corner, even by judging them as an enemy. If you don't push, then they can be a companion.

Process #37: Write a eulogy for your own funeral.

Save fifty percent of compassion for yourself. *Tao* is a selfish *Tao*. If you destroy your companion, you destroy your companion's ability to be God. At the same time, you rob yourself. If you murder one side, you murder yourself. You are a facilitator that selfishly guides your partner to grow to heaven. You can't get to heaven without slowing down to help your partner. Live and let live! Be a good friend so that you maintain peace and harmony. You do not want a gap on your soul. Relationships are simple and complicated at the same time.

Always remember to lighten the fire of light inside the devil. I am the messenger of *Tao*. There are many ways for you to cry. You can cry with tears of anger or joy. Don't judge. Those who know don't talk. Those who talk don't know. A good speaker enjoys a good audience. Holding onto emotion is like shutting down one door after another to the gift from God. The ability to express an emotion is a gift from God! I am real, and as with any real teacher, only people who want to hear a real message can hear. I can kiss anybody's butt if I want to, but I can choose not to do so also.

Once in a while you need a straw boat to borrow the arrows! What you don't have someone else may. Have you ever waited for the right wind to blow from the east? Bring the east and the west together to accomplish *Tao*. Go to your internal knowing. Use your wisdom to stop retarding your spirit. You have the ability to find, accept and search for the true gifts from God. Don't let laziness and stupidity stop you. God creates equal, people always want to destroy equal. When your gift is delivered, don't fantasize. Be honest, real and sincere.

Return to simplicity and continue to be simple yourself. As long as you have a need, the devil will be back. There is a price to pay for that need. There is a need for a material life. The dialectic of that is how to achieve no need. Need and no need are put together for true tranquility. Be a human first. Achieve your best need first. Come to this and you break through on your own. All you have is your own soul and heart to work with.

Process #38: Redo the letter to "I." Also, do a poem called "I." Do not look back at the old poem and letter to "I" before doing it.

Have a conversation with the devil. Be truthful and don't try to be a philosopher. Give nothing less than the truth. Do not soak in the energy, lest it be drained out! Let it be energetically charged, rather than allowing it to deplete you. Before intercourse you have to have the five dragons, the five elements in balance. Making love happens before the actual intercourse. Making soul love is when both individuals are in balance, and they know when making love is right. The dragons dance with each other. The heart celebrates the joy. To make love, you have to be in perfect balance and harmony.

Chapter 53

Master Within

Return to the true nature of self. Cultivate stillness and live for yourself. Enjoy what life presents to you every day, without any attachment. Embrace your true self. Take action to love life and to entertain life. Through cultivation of internal alchemy, you will truly break through *Tao* and unlock the secret to immortality. Not only are you the master of material life, but also you will truly discover the "Master Within." Returning to the immortal life, you will know the true meaning of life. You will truly become immortal among the people on earth and finally an immortal in heaven. When you experience joy, what do you do with it? Let it grow, expand and share it. Learn to do this.

Process #37: Identify the three most joyful events in your life.

Return to your innocence by remembering to be like a child. Open up to wonderment. Be playful. *Taoist* Priests carry a horsetail brush to clear away the dust of their heart. We are always covered by dust and we must remove the dust to come back to our innocence. Pick a joyful time in life and relive it. Choose the most joyful time and go back to that moment to live it. You are reconnecting with the innocent spirit, to re-experience the joy. This brings back innocence and brings the joy. Do this when feeling bad. This is your shelter if you choose.

My first words at three years old were, "When will you stop killing each other?" The village named me *Shen Tong*, "Spirit Child," he who can speak for the Gods. Your spirits are very powerful. Let them out. Allow yourself to lose control a little bit. Why do you have to maintain control all the time? The logical mind wants to maintain control all the time. When you are extraordinary, you feel out of control. This is what your spirit craves. Let your spirit take you where you are supposed to be. When your spirit awakens, it appears in so many ways. Some experience it as a voice, a feeling, as a unity, as a total stillness moment, or your body is out of control. Allow yourself, don't struggle to get back to the human level. During meditation you will experience this moment. The spirit needs these moments. It's a temporary recharge. When spirit awakens it can do something very extraordinary!

I am 14th generation of *Zhang San Feng* branch of *Taoist* wisdom. This book is the five thousand year old message, the five thousand year old Taoist wisdom that I, as humble messenger of the *Tao* carry from East to West for my Grand Master, *Cheng Yu Li*. I bring this message so that the spirit of the East and the spirit of the West may merge, so that the wisdom of the ancient and the intelligence of the modern may merge, much as have the white dragon and the black dragon merged. One becomes two, two becomes three and three becomes ten thousand. And then, ten thousand becomes three, three becomes two, two becomes one, one becomes void and void becomes *Tao*. See and don't see, hear and don't hear, do and don't do. Do nothing and leave nothing undone. Follow nature to death; reverse nature to immortality. *Tao* follows what is nature and then, unites with heaven as one. Return is motion of the *Tao*! You are meant to live a happy life. May you all awaken your master within, may you all enjoy a passion for life.

About the Author

Master Chen

Yun Xiang Tseng, or Master Chen, as he is lovingly called by his students, was born into humble beginnings—a very poor family in a poor village in the Chinese city of Chang Le. Almost prophetically Chang Le means "the longest happiness." Accordingly, though his family was lacking for material riches, Master Chen enjoyed the way that he lived. For the first three years of life, his mother tells that he didn't speak a single word, but that he vigilantly observed his world, taking everything in. At the age of three when he finally began to speak, it soon became apparent that Master Chen was a special child, a child who was able to communicate between the spirit and the human worlds. By the age of four he became somewhat famous throughout the countryside for his ability to act as a medium. Thousands of people traveled to his small village seeking his counsel on spiritual matters. Even the priests at the local Taoist temple commonly requested his presence, asking him questions and beseeching him to pray for the community regarding urgent matters.

At the tender age of six, while tending to his lone cow near a creek at the village edge, young Master Chen was startled by a mystical man with a long beard and dressed in a funny hat, who was making strange hand motions, as though he were playing with a ball. Suddenly this man flicked the imaginary ball into a nearby tree causing the tree to shake and leaves to fall. Though startled, Chen approached the Taoist priest, Master Guo and asked him, "What kind of spooky power do you do that makes the tree shake?" The Taoist priest, who was the Kung Fu Abbott of Wudang Mountain, patted him on the head and responded that he had traveled over a thousand miles in search of him. Master Guo told Chen that he must come with him if he was to learn the power of the magic that he displayed. He asked Chen if he wanted to come. Master Guo had been sent by Chen's eventual spiritual master: Master Li Cheng Yu, who in 1972 was one hundred years old and who lived to be 134 years old before leaving her body. Master Li had told Master Guo where to find Chen, what he would be doing, what he looked like and what he would be wearing. Chen readily agreed to go with Master Guo, so they went to his parents to ask for permission to travel to the Taoist temples of Wudang Mountain.

And so it was that they began the long journey to the temples of Wudang Mountain, a journey spanning three months and a thousand miles by foot. While they traveled, Chen was taught what virtue meant, how to meditate, how to overcome heat and cold and how to survive without food. When they had nothing to eat, sometimes they would eat grass roots or whatever other natural foods were available. Occasionally, they would be invited into someone's home, but more often than not, they would sleep outdoors without a roof or in run down temples. Eventually, one day they arrived at a small broken down temple where Chen saw an elderly lady dressed as a priestess with a Primordial hat and a blue robe. Master Li said to him, "I hear you have come from far away! I knew that you would be coming today child. I have been waiting for you for so long." This is how Chen was introduced to his Master and to the mystical five thousand year old ancient Taoist wisdom of Wudang Mountain. Wudang is one of China's most sacred mountains and is one of the birthplaces of Taoist philosophy.

For the entirety of his childhood, Master Chen knew of no other existence and was trained in the temples of Wudang Mountain. He was taught the ancient wisdom on how to live a happy, long and fruitful life. Through mastering the Taoist arts of Kung Fu, Tai Chi, Qi Gong, internal alchemy and meditation, he realized the secrets of who we are as spiritual people, why we are here on this earth, what our purpose is, and where we are going. He learned the answers to the questions that every religion tries to solve. During his years of training, Master Chen was put through many tests, the toughest of which was when at the age of ten he was sent off to travel in the streets of three provinces, to be a beggar in the middle of the winter for three months. The test was meant to teach him about compassion and humanity. This was during the time of the Cultural Revolution when everybody was wanting for food and everybody was suspicious of strangers. Though he was exposed to extreme hardship and danger he had taken a vow not to use any of the Kung Fu skills that he had learned at the temples. People spat on him and chased dogs after him. At one point he was freezing, starving and near to death. It was then that an old woman who had just a few boiled eggs to her possession out of great compassion gave Chen a couple eggs. Lessons like these taught Master Chen about the innate compassion of human kind.

Upon mastering these ancient arts and wisdom, after years of training and living at the temples, Master Chen was told by Master Li to wait for the right time, for the wind to blow from the East, meaning that he must travel to the West. Master Li had requested that her prodigy travel to the modern world of the West to be the ambassador of Taoist wisdom: to carry this ancient wisdom uniting the yang of eastern philosophy with the yin of modern technology. For over twenty years now, Master Chen has learned the way to communicate this little understood Taoist wisdom of the Eastern world to people in the West.

During this time Master Chen has taught and befriended many of thousands of students.

Wu Dang Tao
The Spiritual Center of Tao in America

Study with Master Chen

Master Chen carries a 700-year-old tradition directly from the Wu Dang Mountains in China. Wu Dang Tao is the spiritual home of the Taoist tradition in the United States.

At Wu Dang Tao, Master Chen has taught Tai Chi, Qi Gong, and other internal martial arts to thousands of students, helping them lead more fulfilling, energetic and powerful lives.

You have the opportunity to study with Master Chen in the martial arts and spiritual practices of Tai Chi, Qi Gong, Wu Ji, and Liang Yi.

Home Study Materials

If you are unable to come to Wu Dang, or if you wish to continue your training after your visit, you may study with Master Chen through a series of videos, CDs, DVDs and other home study materials. Explore the range of products to help you cultivate your Qi energy.

The Master's Blog is a regular source of inspiring thoughts about the practice of internal Wu Dang arts, directly from Master Chen himself.

All of the Wu Dang arts (Qi Gong, Tai Chi, Wu Ji, and Liang Yi) bring great benefits to their practitioners, enhancing their health, mental focus, energy and longevity.

Wu Dang in the West

Master Chen has made it his mission to bring Wu Dang Taoist Arts to the West and to build the first Taoist temple in the United States.

* * *

For more information on workshops, classes, online lectures, home study materials, Master Chen's Blog and much more, please visit www.WuDangTao.com